Building LLMs with LangChain

Master prompt engineering, chaining, and agent development for advanced LLM applications

Martin Dunagan

Copyright © 2024 Martin Dunagan

All rights reserved. No part of this book may be reproduced, stored in a retrieval system, or transmitted, in any form or by any means, electronic, mechanical, photocopying, recording, or otherwise, without the prior written permission of the author, except in the case of brief quotations embodied in critical reviews and certain other noncommercial uses permitted by copyright law.

Table of Contents

Preface..6
Chapter 1: Large Language Models and LangChain......................9
    1.1 What are Large Language Models (LLMs)?....................... 9
    1.2 Capabilities and Limitations of LLMs............................. 12
    1.3 Introducing LangChain..15
    1.4 Setting Up Your Development Environment..................... 23
Chapter 2: Prompt Engineering Fundamentals............................. 28
    2.1 The Art and Science of Prompt Engineering.................... 28
    2.2 Crafting Effective Prompts.. 31
    2.3 Exploring Different Prompt Types.................................. 38
    2.4 Advanced Prompting Techniques................................... 53
Chapter 3: LLM Chains: Building Sequential Workflows.................65
    3.1 Introduction to LLM Chains.. 65
    3.2 Types of Chains... 67
    3.3 Building Chains with LangChain.................................... 78
    3.4 Practical Examples... 83
Chapter 4: Agents and Autonomous Interactions.........................91
    4.1 Rise of LLM Agents... 91
    4.2 Agent Architectures and Use Cases...............................93
    4.3 Building Agents with LangChain.................................. 100
    4.4 Example: Building a Research Agent............................ 103
Chapter 5: Memory and Contextual Awareness......................... 108
    5.1 Why Memory Matters for LLMs....................................108
    5.2 Memory Types in LangChain....................................... 111
    5.3 Integrating Memory into LLM Applications.....................119
    5.4 Example: Building a Chatbot with Memory................... 123
Chapter 6: Case Studies and Practical Examples........................ 127
    6.1 Building a Chatbot with LangChain...............................127
    6.2 Creating a Question-Answering System........................ 131
    6.3 Developing a Code Assistant....................................... 135
    6.4 Generating Personalized Content................................ 138
    6.5 Automating Customer Support..................................... 142

Chapter 7: Advanced Topics...147
    7.1 Evaluation and Fine-tuning of LLM Applications......................147
    7.2 Integrating LLMs with External Data Sources and APIs........... 150
    7.3 Deploying LLM Applications... 154
    7.4 Scaling LLM Applications..156
Chapter 8: The Future of LLMs and LangChain............................. 161
    8.1 Emerging Trends in the LLM Landscape................................. 161
    8.2 Future Directions for LangChain..164
    8.3 Ethical Considerations and Responsible AI.............................. 168
Conclusion... 172

Preface

The world is undergoing a profound transformation, driven by the rise of large language models (LLMs). These powerful AI systems are capable of understanding and generating human-like text, opening up a universe of possibilities across various domains. From writing compelling stories and translating languages to answering complex questions and generating code, LLMs are rapidly changing how we interact with technology and information.

However, harnessing the full potential of LLMs requires more than just accessing these models. It demands a deep understanding of how to effectively communicate with them, orchestrate their capabilities, and integrate them into meaningful applications. This is where LangChain comes in.

LangChain is a powerful and flexible framework designed to simplify the development of LLM-powered applications. It provides a set of tools and abstractions that make it easier to chain LLMs together, integrate them with external data sources, and build autonomous agents that can reason and act in complex environments.

This book is your comprehensive guide to mastering LangChain and building advanced LLM applications. Whether you're a seasoned developer, a data scientist, or an AI enthusiast, this book will equip you with the knowledge and skills you need to leverage the power of LLMs.

What you will learn:

- Fundamentals of LLMs and LangChain: We start with the basics, introducing you to the core concepts of LLMs and the LangChain framework. You'll learn about the different

components of LangChain and how they work together to enable sophisticated LLM applications.
- Prompt Engineering: Master the art of prompt engineering, a crucial skill for effectively communicating with LLMs. You'll learn how to craft prompts that elicit the desired responses, optimize for different tasks, and avoid common pitfalls.
- Chaining LLMs: Discover how to chain LLMs together to create complex workflows and solve intricate problems. We'll explore different chaining techniques and provide practical examples of how to build powerful LLM pipelines.
- Building LLM Agents: Dive into the world of LLM agents, exploring how to design and implement agents that can autonomously interact with their environment, make decisions, and achieve goals.
- Memory and Context: Understand the importance of memory in LLM applications and learn how to integrate different memory mechanisms into your LangChain projects.
- Real-world Applications: Explore a variety of practical use cases and case studies, demonstrating how LangChain can be applied to build chatbots, question-answering systems, code assistants, and more.
- Advanced Topics: Delve into advanced concepts such as evaluating and fine-tuning LLM applications, integrating with external data sources, and deploying LLM applications in production environments.

This book is designed to be both practical and informative. It features numerous code examples, real-world case studies, and best practices to help you get started with LangChain and build your own LLM applications.

We believe that LLMs have the potential to revolutionize many aspects of our lives. With LangChain, you can be at the forefront of this revolution, creating innovative and impactful applications that leverage the power of these incredible technologies.

Chapter 1: Large Language Models and LangChain

1.1 What are Large Language Models (LLMs)?

LLMs are advanced computer programs designed to understand and generate human language. They achieve this through a process called "deep learning," where they are trained on massive datasets of text and code. This training allows them to learn the intricate patterns and structures of language, enabling them to perform a wide range of tasks that were once thought to be exclusive to humans.

How LLMs Work

At the heart of an LLM lies a neural network, a complex structure inspired by the human brain. This network consists of interconnected nodes (like neurons) organized in layers. During training, the LLM processes vast amounts of text data, and the connections between these nodes are adjusted to capture the relationships between words, phrases, and grammatical structures.

One of the key breakthroughs in LLM development is the use of a specific type of neural network architecture called a "transformer." Transformers are particularly good at processing sequential data like language, as they can consider the context of a word by looking at the words that come before and after it. This allows LLMs to understand the meaning of words in a sentence and generate text that is both grammatically correct and contextually relevant.

Training an LLM

Training an LLM is a computationally intensive process. It involves feeding the model massive amounts of text data and adjusting the parameters of the neural network to minimize errors in predicting the next word in a sequence. This process can take weeks or even months, requiring specialized hardware and massive computing power.

The training data itself is crucial. It typically includes books, articles, websites, code, and other forms of text. The quality and diversity of this data directly impact the LLM's capabilities and potential biases.

Examples of LLMs

Several prominent LLMs have emerged in recent years, each with its own strengths and characteristics:

- GPT-3 and GPT-4 (OpenAI): Known for their impressive text generation capabilities and ability to perform a wide range of tasks, from writing stories to answering questions.
- LaMDA (Google): Designed with a focus on dialogue applications, exhibiting strong conversational abilities and a knack for understanding nuances in language.
- PaLM (Google): A more recent model that excels at reasoning tasks and code generation, showcasing the increasing sophistication of LLMs.

Key Concepts

To further understand LLMs, let's explore some key concepts:

- Tokenization: Before an LLM can process text, it needs to break it down into smaller units called "tokens." These tokens can be words, subwords, or even characters, depending on the specific model.

- Embeddings: LLMs represent words and phrases as numerical vectors called "embeddings." These embeddings capture the semantic meaning of words, allowing the model to understand relationships between them.
- Attention Mechanism: This mechanism allows the LLM to focus on the most relevant parts of the input text when generating output. It's like the model is paying attention to the most important words in a sentence to understand its overall meaning.

Code Example (Python with Transformers library)

Here's a simple example of how to use a pre-trained LLM (GPT-2) for text generation using the Hugging Face Transformers library:

Python

```python
from transformers import pipeline

generator = pipeline('text-generation', model='gpt2')

prompt = "Once upon a time, in a land far away,"

generated_text = generator(prompt, max_length=100, num_return_sequences=1)

print(generated_text[0]['generated_text'])
```

This code snippet demonstrates how easily you can leverage pre-trained LLMs to generate text. You provide a starting prompt, and the model continues the story.

Real-World Examples

LLMs are already being used in a variety of applications:

- Chatbots: Providing customer support, answering questions, and engaging in conversations.

- Content creation: Writing articles, generating marketing copy, and creating personalized content.
- Code assistants: Helping developers write code, suggest improvements, and find bugs.
- Translation: Translating text between different languages with increasing accuracy.

As LLMs continue to evolve, we can expect to see even more innovative applications emerge, transforming the way we interact with technology and information.

1.2 Capabilities and Limitations of LLMs

LLMs are undoubtedly powerful tools with a wide range of capabilities. They can perform tasks that were once considered exclusive to humans, pushing the boundaries of what's possible with artificial intelligence. However, it's crucial to recognize their limitations to have realistic expectations and use them responsibly.

Capabilities

Let's break down some of the key capabilities of LLMs:

Text Generation: This is arguably the most impressive capability of LLMs. They can generate human-quality text in various formats, including:

- Creative Writing: Stories, poems, scripts, musical pieces, email, letters, etc.
- Informative Content: Articles, summaries, reports, and even code.
- Personalized Content: Tailored messages, product descriptions, and recommendations.

Language Understanding and Comprehension: LLMs can analyze and understand text, enabling them to:

- Answer Questions: Provide accurate and relevant answers to a wide range of questions, even open-ended or complex ones.
- Summarize Text: Condense lengthy documents into concise summaries.
- Translate Languages: Translate text between multiple languages with increasing accuracy.
- Extract Information: Identify key entities, topics, and relationships in text.

Reasoning and Problem-Solving: While still an area of active research, LLMs are showing promising abilities in:

- Logical Reasoning: Solving logic puzzles and making inferences.
- Mathematical Reasoning: Performing basic mathematical calculations and solving word problems.
- Code Generation: Writing code in various programming languages, completing code snippets, and finding bugs.

Dialogue and Interaction: LLMs are being used to power more natural and engaging conversational interfaces:

- Chatbots: Providing customer support, answering questions, and engaging in casual conversations.
- Virtual Assistants: Helping users with tasks, scheduling appointments, and providing information.

Limitations

Despite their impressive capabilities, LLMs are not without limitations:

- Lack of Common Sense and Real-World Knowledge: LLMs are trained on text data, which doesn't fully capture the nuances of the physical world or human experiences. They

can struggle with tasks that require common sense reasoning or knowledge about everyday objects and events.
- Bias and Ethical Concerns: LLMs can inherit biases present in their training data, leading to outputs that are discriminatory, offensive, or perpetuate harmful stereotypes. Addressing these biases is a critical challenge in LLM development.
- Hallucinations: LLMs can sometimes generate incorrect or nonsensical information, a phenomenon known as "hallucination." This can occur when the model is uncertain or tries to fill in gaps in its knowledge.
- Limited Explainability: It can be difficult to understand why an LLM produces a particular output. This lack of transparency can make it challenging to debug errors or identify biases.
- Computational Cost: Training and deploying LLMs can be computationally expensive, requiring significant resources and energy.

Real-World Examples of Limitations

- Misinformation: An LLM might generate a news article that contains factually incorrect information due to biases or gaps in its knowledge.
- Offensive Content: An LLM trained on biased data might generate responses that are racist, sexist, or otherwise offensive.
- Inaccurate Code: An LLM might generate code that contains syntax errors or doesn't function as intended due to its limited understanding of programming concepts.

Addressing Limitations

Researchers and developers are actively working to address these limitations through various techniques:

- Improving Training Data: Curating more diverse and representative datasets to reduce bias and improve factual accuracy.
- Fine-tuning: Adapting pre-trained LLMs to specific tasks or domains to enhance their performance and reduce errors.
- Reinforcement Learning: Training LLMs to align their outputs with human preferences and values.
- Explainable AI: Developing methods to make LLM decision-making more transparent and understandable.

It's important to remember that LLMs are still a relatively young technology. As research progresses and these limitations are addressed, we can expect LLMs to become even more powerful and versatile tools.

1.3 Introducing LangChain

Think of LangChain as a toolbox that makes it easier to build applications with LLMs. It provides a structured framework for working with LLMs, making it easier to develop applications that leverage their power. Think of it as a toolkit with specialized components designed to interact with LLMs and build more complex systems. Let's explore these core components in detail.

1. Models

At the foundation of LangChain are the **models**. This is where you integrate your chosen Large Language Model. LangChain supports a wide variety of models, including:

- OpenAI Models: GPT-3, GPT-4, Codex
- Hugging Face Hub Models: Access to a vast collection of open-source LLMs.
- Other LLMs: LangChain is constantly expanding its support for other LLMs, including those from Cohere, AI21 Labs, and more.

LangChain provides a standardized interface for interacting with these different models, abstracting away the complexities of each specific API. This allows you to easily switch between models or even combine them in your applications.

Code Example (Python with LangChain)

Python

```python
from langchain.llms import OpenAI
# Initialize the OpenAI LLM (requires an API key)
llm = OpenAI(temperature=0.7)
# Generate text from the LLM
text = llm("Tell me a short story about a cat who goes on an adventure.")
print(text)
```

In this example, we initialize an OpenAI LLM using LangChain and then use it to generate a short story.

2. Prompts

Prompts are the instructions or inputs you provide to an LLM to guide its output. They are essential for eliciting the desired response from the model. Think of prompts as the questions or tasks you give to the LLM.

LangChain provides a PromptTemplate class to create and manage prompts effectively. This allows you to:

- Define Templates: Create reusable prompt templates with placeholders for variables.
- Format Inputs: Dynamically fill in the placeholders with specific values.
- Manage Variations: Experiment with different prompt variations to optimize performance.

Code Example (Python with LangChain)

```python
from langchain.prompts import PromptTemplate
template = """
You are a helpful assistant that translates English to French.
Translate the following phrase: {text}
"""
prompt = PromptTemplate(
    input_variables=["text"],
    template=template,
)
# Format the prompt with a specific input
formatted_prompt = prompt.format(text="Hello, how are you?")
print(formatted_prompt)
```

This example demonstrates how to create a prompt template for translation and then format it with a specific phrase.

3. Chains

Chains enable you to combine multiple LLMs or other components in a sequence to perform more complex tasks. They allow you to create workflows where the output of one step becomes the input for the next.

LangChain offers various types of chains:

- Sequential Chains: Execute a series of steps in a specific order.
- Router Chains: Direct the flow of execution based on conditions or rules.
- Transform Chains: Modify or transform the output of one step before passing it to the next.

Code Example (Python with LangChain)

Python

```
from langchain.chains import LLMChain
from langchain.prompts import PromptTemplate
from langchain.llms import OpenAI
# Define the prompt template
template = """
You are a helpful assistant that summarizes text.
Summarize the following text: {text}
"""
prompt_template = PromptTemplate(input_variables=["text"], template=template)
# Initialize the LLM chain
llm = OpenAI(temperature=0)
chain = LLMChain(llm=llm, prompt=prompt_template)
# Run the chain with some input text
text = "This is a long document about the history of artificial intelligence..."
summary = chain.run(text)
print(summary)
```

This example shows a simple chain that summarizes text using an LLM.

4. Agents

Agents take automation to the next level. They allow LLMs to interact with their environment, gather information, and make decisions to achieve a specific goal. LangChain provides tools for building agents that can:

- Access Tools: Interact with external APIs, databases, or other sources of information.
- Plan Actions: Determine the best course of action based on the current context.
- Execute Actions: Carry out actions to achieve the desired outcome.

Example: A research agent that can browse the web, access databases, and synthesize information to answer complex questions.

5. Memory

Memory is a crucial component for building conversational applications with LLMs. It allows the LLM to retain information from previous interactions, enabling more context-aware and coherent responses.

LangChain offers various memory types:

- ConversationBufferMemory: Stores the entire conversation history.
- ConversationSummaryMemory: Keeps a summarized version of the conversation.
- Entity Memory: Remembers specific entities and their attributes.

Example: A chatbot that remembers your name and previous questions, providing a more personalized experience.

By understanding these core components – Models, Prompts, Chains, Agents, and Memory – you can unlock the full potential of LangChain and build sophisticated LLM applications that can understand, reason, and interact with the world around them.

Why LangChain?

LangChain has quickly emerged as a powerful and versatile framework for building applications with Large Language Models (LLMs). It offers a number of advantages that simplify the development process, enhance application capabilities, and promote best practices in LLM development.

Here's a breakdown of the key reasons why developers and researchers are choosing LangChain:

1. Simplified Development

Working with LLMs can be complex, especially when dealing with different model providers, APIs, and data formats. LangChain simplifies this process by providing:

- Standardized Interface: LangChain offers a consistent and intuitive interface for interacting with various LLMs, regardless of their underlying architecture or provider. This abstraction layer allows you to easily switch between models or even combine them without having to write custom code for each one.
- Modular Components: LangChain provides a set of modular components, such as prompts, chains, and agents, that you can easily assemble and configure to build your applications. This modularity promotes code reusability and reduces development time.

- Helpful Utilities: LangChain includes helpful utilities for common tasks like prompt management, output parsing, and data loading, further streamlining the development process.

2. Enhanced Capabilities

LangChain enables you to build more sophisticated LLM applications by providing:

- Chain Composition: You can chain together multiple LLMs or other processing steps to create complex workflows. This allows you to break down complex tasks into smaller, manageable steps and leverage the strengths of different models.
- Agent Development: LangChain provides tools for building LLM-powered agents that can interact with their environment, gather information, and make decisions. This opens up possibilities for creating applications that can automate tasks, perform research, and engage in more dynamic interactions.
- External Data Integration: You can easily connect your LLMs to external data sources, such as APIs, databases, and knowledge graphs. This allows you to build applications that can access and process real-world information, making them more informative and useful.

3. Best Practices and Community Support

LangChain promotes best practices in LLM development by:

- Encouraging Modularity: The modular design of LangChain encourages you to write cleaner, more maintainable code.
- Promoting Reusability: You can reuse components and chains across different projects, saving time and effort.
- Fostering a Strong Community: LangChain has a growing and active community of users and developers who

contribute to the project, share knowledge, and provide support.

Real-World Examples

Here are some examples of how LangChain is being used in real-world applications:

- Chatbots: Companies are using LangChain to build more sophisticated chatbots that can understand complex questions, provide personalized responses, and even complete tasks.
- Content Creation: Marketing teams are using LangChain to generate high-quality content, such as articles, social media posts, and product descriptions, at scale.
- Code Assistants: Developers are using LangChain to build code assistants that can help them write code faster, identify bugs, and suggest improvements.
- Data Analysis: Analysts are using LangChain to build tools that can analyze large datasets, extract insights, and generate reports.

By providing a robust framework, simplifying development, and promoting best practices, LangChain empowers developers to build innovative and impactful applications that leverage the full potential of LLMs.

1.4 Setting Up Your Development Environment

Before we embark on our journey of building LLM applications with LangChain, we need to prepare your development environment. This involves setting up the necessary tools and dependencies to write and execute code. Don't worry, it's a straightforward process, and I'll guide you through it step-by-step.

1. Install Python

LangChain is a Python library, so the first step is to ensure you have Python installed on your system. If you're not sure whether you have Python installed or which version, you can check by opening your terminal or command prompt and typing:

Bash

python --version

If Python is installed, this command will display the version number. If not, you'll need to download and install it from the official Python website (python.org). I recommend using the latest stable version of Python (3.10 or later).

2. Install LangChain

Once you have Python installed, you can install LangChain using pip, the Python package installer. Open your terminal or command prompt and type:

Bash

pip install langchain

This command will download and install the latest version of LangChain, along with its core dependencies.

3. Choose an LLM

Next, you need to decide which Large Language Model (LLM) you want to use for your applications. LangChain supports a wide variety of LLMs, each with its own strengths and characteristics. Some popular choices include:

- OpenAI Models (GPT-3, GPT-4): These models are known for their impressive text generation capabilities and are accessible through the OpenAI API.
- Hugging Face Hub Models: This platform provides access to a vast collection of open-source LLMs, many of which can be used for free.
- Other LLMs: LangChain also supports models from other providers, such as Cohere, AI21 Labs, and more.

You'll need to install the necessary packages to interact with your chosen LLM. For example, if you're using OpenAI models, you'll need to install the openai package:

Bash

pip install openai

4. API Keys and Authentication

If you're using a cloud-based LLM, such as those provided by OpenAI, you'll need to obtain an API key to access the model. This key acts as your authentication credential and allows you to make requests to the API.

You can typically find instructions on how to obtain an API key on the provider's website. Once you have the key, you'll need to configure your environment to use it. This might involve setting an environment variable or passing the key as an argument to your LangChain code.

5. Choose a Code Editor or IDE

To write and execute your LangChain code, you'll need a code editor or an Integrated Development Environment (IDE). Some popular choices include:

- VS Code: A versatile and lightweight code editor with excellent Python support.

- PyCharm: A full-featured IDE specifically designed for Python development.
- Jupyter Notebooks: Interactive notebooks that are great for experimenting with code and visualizing data.

Choose the editor that best suits your preferences and workflow.

6. (Optional) Set Up a Virtual Environment

It's generally a good practice to create a virtual environment for your LangChain projects. This isolates your project's dependencies from other Python projects on your system, preventing conflicts and ensuring a clean development environment.

You can create a virtual environment using the venv module in Python:

Bash

```
python -m venv my_langchain_env
```

This will create a new virtual environment named my_langchain_env. You'll then need to activate it before installing any packages or running your code.

Example: Setting Up for OpenAI Models

Here's an example of how to set up your environment to use OpenAI models with LangChain:

1. Install Python: Ensure you have Python 3.10 or later installed.
2. Install LangChain and OpenAI:

Bash

```
pip install langchain openai
```

3. Obtain an OpenAI API Key: Sign up for an OpenAI account and generate an API key.
4. Set the Environment Variable:

```Bash
export OPENAI_API_KEY="your_api_key_here"
```

5. Write and Run Your Code:

```Python
from langchain.llms import OpenAI

llm = OpenAI(temperature=0.7)

text = llm("Tell me a joke.")

print(text)
```

That's it! You've now set up your development environment and are ready to start building LLM applications with LangChain.

This is just a basic setup. As you explore more advanced features and integrate with other tools, you might need to install additional packages or configure your environment further. However, this foundation will get you started on your LangChain journey.

Chapter 2: Prompt Engineering Fundamentals

Prompt engineering is the art and science of crafting effective inputs, or "prompts," to guide LLMs toward generating the desired outputs. It's a critical skill for anyone working with LLMs, as the quality of your prompts directly impacts the quality of the results you get.

Think of it like giving directions to someone. If your directions are vague or ambiguous, they might end up lost or at the wrong destination. But if your directions are clear, concise, and specific, they'll reach their destination with ease. The same principle applies to LLMs: the better your prompts, the better the responses.

2.1 The Art and Science of Prompt Engineering

Prompt engineering is a fascinating field that blends creativity with technical expertise. It's about finding the sweet spot where human intuition meets the capabilities of powerful language models. Let's explore what makes prompt engineering so unique.

At its core, prompt engineering involves crafting effective inputs, or "prompts," to guide Large Language Models (LLMs) toward generating the desired outputs. It's the bridge between your intentions and the LLM's ability to process and generate language.

Think of it like this: you have a powerful tool in your hands (the LLM), but it needs clear instructions to perform the task you have in mind. Prompt engineering is about providing those instructions in a way that the LLM can understand and act upon effectively.

The "Art" in Prompt Engineering

The "art" of prompt engineering lies in the ability to understand the nuances of language and how LLMs interpret different phrasing, styles, and tones. It's about finding the right words and structure to elicit the desired response.

This involves:

- Creativity: Exploring different approaches and experimenting with various prompt structures to discover what works best for a particular task and LLM.
- Intuition: Developing a sense of how the LLM might interpret your prompt and adjusting your approach accordingly.
- Empathy: Putting yourself in the "shoes" of the LLM and trying to understand how it might perceive the information and instructions you provide.

The "Science" in Prompt Engineering

The "science" of prompt engineering involves a more systematic and analytical approach. It's about applying principles and techniques to optimize prompts for specific goals.

This includes:

- Understanding LLM Behavior: Analyzing how different prompt variations affect the output and identifying patterns in the LLM's responses.
- Experimentation: Systematically testing different prompt structures, formats, and parameters to measure their impact on the generated output.
- Optimization: Refining prompts based on experimental results to improve accuracy, relevance, and overall quality.
- Evaluation: Establishing metrics to measure the effectiveness of prompts and track progress over time.

Why is Prompt Engineering Important?

Prompt engineering plays a crucial role in:

- Improving Output Quality: Well-crafted prompts lead to more accurate, relevant, and coherent outputs from LLMs.
- Controlling LLM Behavior: Prompts can be used to steer the LLM toward specific styles, tones, or formats, ensuring the generated content aligns with your needs.
- Unlocking LLM Potential: By understanding how to communicate effectively with LLMs, you can unlock their full capabilities and achieve a wider range of tasks.

Real-World Examples

- Content Creation: A marketing team uses prompt engineering to guide an LLM to generate product descriptions that are informative, engaging, and persuasive.
- Chatbots: A customer support team uses prompt engineering to train a chatbot to provide helpful and accurate responses to common customer queries.
- Code Generation: A software developer uses prompt engineering to instruct an LLM to generate code snippets that meet specific requirements and coding standards.

Prompt Engineering in Action

Let's look at a simple example. Suppose you want an LLM to write a short story about a cat. Here are two different prompts:

Prompt 1: "Write a story about a cat."

Prompt 2: "Write a humorous short story about a mischievous cat named Whiskers who gets lost in a library and causes chaos among the bookshelves."

The second prompt is more specific and provides more context, which is likely to result in a more engaging and imaginative story. This illustrates how prompt engineering can significantly influence the output of an LLM.

As you can see, prompt engineering is a multifaceted discipline that requires both creativity and analytical thinking. By mastering the art and science of prompt engineering, you can harness the power of LLMs to achieve remarkable results.

2.2 Crafting Effective Prompts

You're getting to the heart of good prompting now! Clarity, specificity, and context are like the pillars of effective communication with LLMs. Let's discuss each of these and see how they contribute to getting the best results.

Clarity

When crafting prompts for LLMs, clarity is paramount. Remember, you're essentially giving instructions to a very sophisticated computer program. To ensure the LLM understands your intent, your prompts need to be:

- Unambiguous: Avoid words or phrases that could have multiple interpretations. Be direct and precise in your language.
- Concise: Get straight to the point and avoid unnecessary complexity. LLMs can handle lengthy prompts, but conciseness often leads to better results.
- Well-Structured: Organize your prompt in a logical manner, using clear headings, bullet points, or other formatting elements to improve readability.

Examples of Clarity

- Vague: "Write something about history."
- Clear: "Write a short essay about the impact of the Industrial Revolution on European society."
- Vague: "Tell me about that book."
- Clear: "Summarize the main themes in 'To Kill a Mockingbird' by Harper Lee."

Specificity

Specificity is crucial for guiding the LLM toward the desired output. The more specific your instructions, the better the LLM can understand your expectations and generate relevant responses.

Think of it like this: if you ask a friend to "get you something to eat," they might come back with anything. But if you ask for "a veggie burger with no onions and extra pickles," they have a much clearer idea of what you want.

Examples of Specificity

- General: "Summarize this article."
- Specific: "Summarize this article in three bullet points, focusing on the key findings related to climate change."
- General: "Write a poem."
- Specific: "Write a sonnet about the beauty of nature in the springtime, using vivid imagery and metaphors."

Context

Providing context helps the LLM understand the background and purpose of your request, leading to more accurate and relevant responses. It's like giving the LLM the bigger picture so it can fill in the details appropriately.

Examples of Context

- No Context: "Translate this sentence."
- Context: "Translate this sentence from Spanish to English, ensuring that the translation captures the formal tone of the original text."
- No Context: "Write a song."

- Context: "Write a folk song about the struggles of a migrant worker, using a melancholic melody and lyrics that evoke a sense of longing for home."

Real-World Example

Let's say you're building a chatbot for a customer support website. You want the chatbot to be able to answer questions about a specific product. To ensure the chatbot provides accurate and relevant information, you would provide context in the prompt, such as:

- Product Information: A detailed description of the product, its features, and specifications.
- Target Audience: Information about the typical customer who might use this product.
- Common Questions: A list of frequently asked questions about the product.

By providing this context, you equip the chatbot with the knowledge it needs to answer customer questions effectively.

Clarity, Specificity, and Context in Code

While these principles are primarily about how you write your prompts, they can sometimes be reinforced with code. For instance, if you're using LangChain's PromptTemplate, you can enforce specificity by defining the input_variables that must be provided:

Python

```python
from langchain.prompts import PromptTemplate

template = """
You are a helpful assistant that writes product descriptions.
```

```
Write a description for the following product:
Product Name: {product_name}
Key Features: {key_features}
Target Audience: {target_audience}
"""

prompt = PromptTemplate(
    input_variables=["product_name", "key_features", "target_audience"],
    template=template,
)
```

This code ensures that anyone using this template *must* provide the product name, key features, and target audience, thus enforcing specificity in the prompt.

By applying the principles of clarity, specificity, and context, you can craft effective prompts that guide LLMs toward generating high-quality, relevant, and accurate outputs. Remember, clear communication is key to unlocking the full potential of these powerful language models.

Prompt Templates and Best Practices

Think of prompt templates as blueprints for your prompts. They provide a structured format with placeholders for variables, allowing you to generate a variety of prompts by simply filling in those placeholders with different values.

Benefits of Using Prompt Templates

- Consistency: Templates ensure that your prompts follow a consistent structure and include all the necessary

information. This helps to reduce errors and improve the reliability of LLM outputs.
- Efficiency: Templates save you time and effort by eliminating the need to write every prompt from scratch. You can reuse templates for similar tasks, making your workflow more efficient.
- Flexibility: Templates allow you to easily experiment with different prompt variations by changing the values of the variables. This makes it easier to find the optimal prompt for a given task.
- Maintainability: If you need to update your prompts, you only need to modify the template, and the changes will be reflected in all the prompts generated from it.

Creating Prompt Templates with LangChain

LangChain provides a convenient way to create and manage prompt templates using the PromptTemplate class.

Code Example (Python with LangChain)

Python

```python
from langchain.prompts import PromptTemplate
# Define the template
template = """
You are a helpful assistant that writes stories for children.
Write a short story about a {animal} who goes on an adventure to {place}.
"""
# Create a PromptTemplate object
prompt_template = PromptTemplate(
    input_variables=["animal", "place"],
```

```
    template=template,
)
# Generate prompts by filling in the variables
prompt1 = prompt_template.format(animal="dog",
place="the moon")
prompt2 = prompt_template.format(animal="cat",
place="the jungle")
print(prompt1)
print(prompt2)
```

This code defines a template for writing children's stories. You can then generate different prompts by providing values for the animal and place variables.

Best Practices for Prompt Engineering

Beyond using templates, there are several best practices you can follow to improve your prompt engineering skills:

- Start Simple, Then Iterate: Begin with a simple prompt and gradually add more complexity or constraints as needed. Experiment with different variations and analyze the results to refine your prompts iteratively.
- Give Clear Instructions: Be explicit about what you want the LLM to do. Use action verbs and specific keywords to guide its behavior.
- Provide Examples: Including examples in your prompt can help the LLM understand the desired output format or style.
- Set the Tone: Specify the desired tone for the output (e.g., formal, informal, humorous, informative).
- Control the Length: If you need a specific output length, specify it in your prompt (e.g., "Write a summary in no more than 100 words").

- Break Down Complex Tasks: For complex tasks, consider breaking them down into smaller subtasks and using multiple prompts or chains.
- Be Mindful of Bias: Be aware of potential biases in the LLM's training data and take steps to mitigate their effects in your prompts and outputs.
- Evaluate and Refine: Continuously evaluate the effectiveness of your prompts and refine them based on feedback and observations.

Real-World Example

A company wants to use an LLM to generate personalized email subject lines for their marketing campaigns. They create a prompt template that includes variables for the recipient's name, the product being promoted, and the tone of the email:

- **Subject: {Recipient Name}, {Tone} about {Product Name}?**

By filling in these variables with different values, they can generate a variety of subject lines tailored to different customer segments and campaign goals.

Incorporating prompt templates and following best practices, you can streamline your prompt engineering workflow, improve the quality of your prompts, and ultimately get better results from your LLM applications. Remember, prompt engineering is an iterative process. Continuously experiment, evaluate, and refine your prompts to achieve the best possible outcomes.

2.3 Exploring Different Prompt Types

LLMs can be used for a wide range of tasks, and the type of prompt you use will depend on the specific goal you're trying to achieve. Here are some common prompt types:

Question Answering

At its simplest, question answering involves presenting an LLM with a question and getting a relevant and accurate answer in response. However, there's more to it than just asking a question. Effective prompt engineering can significantly improve the accuracy, completeness, and conciseness of the answers you receive.

Types of Questions

LLMs can handle a wide range of question types, including:

- Factual Questions: Questions with clear, objective answers that can be found in knowledge sources.

    Example: "What is the capital of Australia?"

- Open-ended Questions: Questions that require more elaborate answers and may have multiple valid perspectives.

    Example: "What are the ethical implications of artificial intelligence?"

- Complex Questions: Questions that involve multiple steps or require the LLM to synthesize information from different sources.

    Example: "Compare and contrast the economic policies of the United States and China."

Prompting Techniques for Question Answering

Here are some techniques to improve your question-answering prompts:

- Be Specific and Clear: Clearly state the question you want the LLM to answer. Avoid ambiguity or vagueness.

    Instead of: "Tell me about the moon."

Use: "What are the main phases of the moon and how long does each phase last?"

- Provide Context (if necessary): If the question requires background information or refers to a specific document or topic, provide that context in the prompt.

  Example: "Based on the article provided, what are the author's main arguments in favor of renewable energy?"

- Specify the Desired Format: If you want the answer in a specific format (e.g., bullet points, a table, a paragraph), state that in the prompt.

  Example: "List three key benefits of regular exercise."

- Constrain the Answer Length: If you need a concise answer, specify a word or character limit.

  Example: "In one sentence, explain the difference between a simile and a metaphor."

- Ask for Sources or Evidence: To improve the reliability of the answer, ask the LLM to provide sources or evidence to support its claims.

  Example: "What are the main causes of climate change? Provide scientific evidence to support your answer."

Code Example (Python with LangChain)

```python
Python

from langchain.llms import OpenAI

from langchain.prompts import PromptTemplate

# Define the prompt template

template = """
```

```
You are a helpful assistant that answers
questions about history.

Question: {question}
"""

prompt_template = PromptTemplate(

    input_variables=["question"],

    template=template,

)

# Initialize the LLM

llm = OpenAI(temperature=0)

# Generate a prompt with a specific question

prompt = prompt_template.format(question="What were the main causes of World War I?")

# Get the answer from the LLM

answer = llm(prompt)

print(answer)
```

Real-World Examples

- Customer Support: Companies use LLM-powered chatbots to answer customer questions about products, services, or policies.
- Education: LLMs can be used to create interactive learning environments where students can ask questions and receive personalized feedback.

- Research: Researchers use LLMs to quickly access and synthesize information from vast amounts of text data.
- Content Creation: Writers use LLMs to answer questions, generate ideas, and fact-check their work.

Challenges and Considerations

While LLMs are powerful question-answering tools, there are some challenges to keep in mind:

- Hallucinations: LLMs can sometimes generate incorrect or nonsensical answers, especially for questions that require complex reasoning or knowledge that is not well-represented in their training data.
- Bias: LLMs can reflect biases present in their training data, leading to answers that are inaccurate or unfair.
- Source Reliability: LLMs may not always be able to identify reliable sources or distinguish between credible and non-credible information.

By understanding these challenges and applying effective prompt engineering techniques, you can improve the accuracy and reliability of LLM-powered question-answering systems.

Text Summarization

Text summarization is the process of creating a shorter version of a longer text while preserving its key information and meaning. LLMs excel at this task, as they can analyze and understand the relationships between different parts of a text to identify the most important information.

Types of Text Summarization

There are two main types of text summarization:

- Extractive Summarization: This involves selecting and extracting sentences or phrases directly from the original

text to form the summary. It's like highlighting the most important sentences in a document.
- Abstractive Summarization: This involves generating new sentences that capture the essence of the original text, even if those sentences don't appear verbatim in the original. It's like paraphrasing and condensing the information.

LLMs are capable of both extractive and abstractive summarization, and the type of summary you get can be influenced by your prompt.

Prompting Techniques for Text Summarization

Here are some techniques to improve your text summarization prompts:

- Be Clear About the Desired Length: Specify the desired length of the summary (e.g., word count, sentence count, percentage of original text).

    Example: "Summarize this article in 100 words."

- Specify the Type of Summary: Indicate whether you want an extractive or abstractive summary.

    Example: "Provide a concise abstractive summary of this research paper."

- Focus on Key Information: Guide the LLM to focus on specific aspects of the text, such as the main arguments, key findings, or conclusions.

    Example: "Summarize the main arguments presented in this debate, focusing on the opposing viewpoints."

- Specify the Target Audience: If the summary is intended for a specific audience, mention that in the prompt.

    Example: "Summarize this scientific article for a general audience."

- Provide Context (if necessary): If the text is part of a larger context (e.g., a book chapter, a series of articles), provide that context in the prompt.

    Example: "Summarize this chapter in the context of the overall argument of the book."

Code Example (Python with LangChain)

```python
from langchain.llms import OpenAI
from langchain.prompts import PromptTemplate

# Define the prompt template
template = """
You are a helpful assistant that summarizes text.
Summarize the following article:
{article_text}
Summary:
"""
prompt_template = PromptTemplate(
    input_variables=["article_text"],
    template=template,
)
# Initialize the LLM
llm = OpenAI(temperature=0)
```

```
# Load the article text

with open("article.txt", "r") as f:

    article_text = f.read()

# Generate the prompt

prompt = prompt_template.format(article_text=article_text)

# Get the summary from the LLM

summary = llm(prompt)

print(summary)
```

Real-World Examples

- News Aggregation: News websites use LLMs to generate summaries of articles, allowing readers to quickly grasp the main points.
- Document Analysis: Businesses use LLMs to summarize lengthy reports, contracts, or legal documents.
- Academic Research: Researchers use LLMs to summarize research papers and identify key findings.
- Social Media Monitoring: Companies use LLMs to summarize social media conversations and identify trends.

Challenges and Considerations

- Maintaining Accuracy: Ensuring that the summary accurately reflects the original text can be challenging, especially for complex or nuanced topics.
- Handling Bias: LLMs can introduce biases into summaries if they are not carefully trained and evaluated.
- Preserving Important Details: It can be difficult to ensure that the summary includes all the important details while remaining concise.

Understanding these challenges and applying effective prompt engineering techniques, you can improve the quality and reliability of LLM-generated text summaries.

Code Generation

Code generation is the process of using LLMs to automatically generate code in various programming languages. This can range from simple code snippets to complete functions, classes, or even entire programs. LLMs achieve this by learning the patterns and structures of code from massive datasets of code examples.

Why is Code Generation Useful?

- Increased Productivity: Code generation can significantly speed up the development process by automating repetitive tasks and reducing the amount of code developers need to write manually.
- Improved Accuracy: LLMs can help reduce errors and improve code quality by generating code that adheres to best practices and coding standards.
- Accessibility: Code generation can make programming more accessible to people with less coding experience, allowing them to express their ideas in natural language and have the LLM translate them into code.
- New Possibilities: Code generation opens up new possibilities for creative coding and allows developers to explore new programming paradigms.

Prompting Techniques for Code Generation

Here are some techniques to improve your code generation prompts:

- Be Specific About the Task: Clearly describe the functionality you want the code to perform. The more specific you are, the better the LLM can understand your intent.

Instead of: "Write some Python code."

Use: "Write a Python function that takes a list of numbers as input and returns the sum of all the even numbers in the list."

- Specify the Programming Language: Clearly state the programming language you want the code to be generated in.

  Example: "Generate JavaScript code that creates an interactive map."

- Provide Context and Constraints: If there are specific libraries, frameworks, or coding styles you want the LLM to use, mention them in the prompt.

  Example: "Write a React component that displays a list of products, using the Material UI library for styling."

- Include Examples (if helpful): Providing examples of similar code or input-output pairs can help the LLM understand the desired structure and functionality.

  Example: "Generate Python code that converts temperature from Celsius to Fahrenheit. Here's an example: convert_temperature(25) # Output: 77.0"

- **Test and Refine:** Always test the generated code and refine your prompt if necessary. LLMs can sometimes generate code with errors or unexpected behavior.

Code Example (Python with LangChain)

```python
from langchain.llms import OpenAI
from langchain.prompts import PromptTemplate
# Define the prompt template
```

```python
template = """

You are a helpful assistant that writes Python code.

Write a Python function that {function_description}.

"""

prompt_template = PromptTemplate(
    input_variables=["function_description"],
    template=template,
)

# Initialize the LLM
llm = OpenAI(temperature=0)

# Generate a prompt with a specific function description
prompt = prompt_template.format(
    function_description="takes a string as input and returns the number of vowels in the string"
)

# Get the code from the LLM
code = llm(prompt)
print(code)

# Execute the code (be cautious when executing code from LLMs)
```

```
exec(code)

# Now you can call the function:
count_vowels("hello world")
```

Real-World Examples

- Code Completion: IDEs use LLMs to suggest code completions, helping developers write code faster.
- Bug Detection: LLMs can be used to analyze code and identify potential bugs or vulnerabilities.
- Code Translation: LLMs can translate code from one programming language to another.
- Code Documentation: LLMs can generate documentation for code, making it easier to understand and maintain.
- Web Development: LLMs can generate code for website layouts, interactive elements, and data fetching.

Challenges and Considerations

- Code Correctness: While LLMs can generate impressive code, it's important to thoroughly test and review the code before using it in production.
- Security Risks: LLMs can sometimes generate code with security vulnerabilities if they are not trained on secure coding practices.
- Understanding Complex Logic: LLMs may struggle with generating code for complex algorithms or tasks that require deep domain expertise.

Creative Writing

You're venturing into the domain where LLMs truly shine! Creative writing is where these models can unleash their imaginative potential. Let's explore how you can guide them to produce captivating stories, poems, and more.

The Creative Potential of LLMs

LLMs have a remarkable ability to generate creative text formats, including:

- **Stories:** Short stories, novels, fan fiction, and even screenplays.
- **Poems:** Sonnets, haikus, free verse, and other poetic forms.
- **Scripts:** Dialogue for plays, movies, or video games.
- **Musical Pieces:** Lyrics and melodies for songs.
- **Other Creative Text Formats:** Letters, emails, social media posts, and more.

This creative potential stems from the LLMs' ability to learn patterns in language, understand different writing styles, and generate text that is both original and engaging.

Prompting Techniques for Creative Writing

Here are some techniques to improve your creative writing prompts:

- Provide a Seed or Starting Point: Give the LLM a creative starting point, such as a character, a setting, or a plot idea.

    Example: "Write a story about a young witch who discovers a hidden portal in her backyard."

- Specify the Genre or Style: Indicate the desired genre (e.g., fantasy, science fiction, romance) or writing style (e.g., humorous, dark, suspenseful).

    Example: "Write a science fiction story in the style of Isaac Asimov."

- Set the Tone and Mood: Describe the desired tone and mood of the piece (e.g., lighthearted, melancholic, mysterious).

    Example: "Write a poem about loss and grief, with a somber and reflective tone."

- Use Constraints and Challenges: Introduce creative constraints or challenges to encourage the LLM to think outside the box.

    Example: "Write a story in which all the characters are animals who can talk."

- Provide Examples or Inspiration: Share examples of similar creative works or provide inspirational prompts to guide the LLM's creative process.

    Example: "Write a poem inspired by the works of Emily Dickinson."

- Iterate and Refine: Don't be afraid to experiment with different prompts and refine them based on the LLM's output. The creative process often involves trial and error.

Code Example (Python with LangChain)

```python
from langchain.llms import OpenAI
from langchain.prompts import PromptTemplate

# Define the prompt template

template = """

You are a helpful assistant that writes creative content.

Write a {genre} story about {story_idea}.

"""

prompt_template = PromptTemplate(
    input_variables=["genre", "story_idea"],
```

```python
    template=template,
)

# Initialize the LLM
llm = OpenAI(temperature=0.8)  # Higher temperature for more creativity

# Generate a prompt with specific inputs
prompt = prompt_template.format(
    genre="fantasy",
    story_idea="a knight who embarks on a quest to find a magical sword",
)

# Get the story from the LLM
story = llm(prompt)
print(story)
```

Real-World Examples

- Storytelling: Authors and writers use LLMs to generate story ideas, develop characters, and overcome writer's block.
- Entertainment: Game developers use LLMs to create dynamic and engaging dialogue for video game characters.
- Marketing and Advertising: Marketing teams use LLMs to generate creative content for advertisements, social media posts, and product descriptions.
- Art and Music: Artists and musicians use LLMs to generate lyrics, poems, scripts, and even musical compositions.

Challenges and Considerations

- Originality and Plagiarism: Ensuring the originality of LLM-generated creative content can be a challenge. It's important to be aware of potential plagiarism issues and use tools to check for originality.
- Ethical Concerns: LLMs can sometimes generate content that is offensive, harmful, or biased. It's important to use these tools responsibly and ethically.
- Controlling the Creative Process: While you can guide the LLM's creative process through prompts, you don't have complete control over the output. Be prepared for unexpected and surprising results.

Understanding these challenges and applying effective prompt engineering techniques, you can unleash the creative potential of LLMs and explore new frontiers in storytelling, poetry, and other forms of artistic expression.

2.4 Advanced Prompting Techniques

As you become more comfortable with prompt engineering, you can explore more advanced techniques to further improve the quality and control of LLM outputs. Let's explore how prompt variations and dynamic prompts can add another layer of sophistication to your prompt engineering.

Prompt Variations

Think of prompt variations as trying different approaches to communicate the same basic idea to the LLM. It's like explaining something to someone in different ways until you find the explanation that clicks best.

Why use prompt variations?

- Explore Different Perspectives: Slight changes in wording or structure can lead the LLM to generate different outputs, offering you a wider range of options.
- Optimize for Specific Goals: By experimenting with variations, you can find the prompt that best achieves your specific goals, whether it's accuracy, creativity, or conciseness.
- Overcome Limitations: If the LLM isn't producing the desired output, trying variations can help you overcome its limitations or biases.

Types of Prompt Variations

- Rephrasing: Try rephrasing your instructions using different words or sentence structures.

    Example: Instead of "Write a poem about a tree," try "Compose a poetic tribute to a majestic oak."

- Adding Constraints: Introduce constraints to narrow down the possibilities and guide the LLM toward a specific type of output.

    Example: "Write a short story about a detective solving a mystery, but the story must take place in a futuristic city and involve robots."

- Changing the Order: Reorder the elements in your prompt to see if it affects the output.

    Example: Instead of "Summarize this article and then translate it into Spanish," try "Translate this article into Spanish and then provide a summary."

- Adjusting the Tone: Experiment with different tones (e.g., formal, informal, humorous) to see how it influences the LLM's response.

Example: "Write a formal letter to the editor about climate change" vs. "Write a passionate blog post about the urgency of addressing climate change."

Dynamic Prompts

Dynamic prompts take things a step further by allowing you to generate prompts that change based on user input or previous interactions. This adds a level of interactivity and adaptability to your LLM applications.

How Dynamic Prompts Work

Dynamic prompts typically involve:

- Variables: Using variables or placeholders in your prompt templates that can be filled in with different values at runtime.
- Conditional Logic: Using conditional statements or rules to determine which parts of the prompt to include or modify based on certain conditions.
- User Input: Incorporating user input or feedback to adjust the prompt and guide the LLM's response.

Code Example (Python with LangChain)

```python
Python

from langchain.llms import OpenAI

from langchain.prompts import PromptTemplate

# Define the prompt template

template = """

You are a helpful assistant that writes different kinds of creative text formats.
```

```python
Write a {style} poem about {subject}.

The user has provided the following additional instructions: {user_instructions}
"""

prompt_template = PromptTemplate(
    input_variables=["style", "subject", "user_instructions"],
    template=template,
)

# Get user input

style = input("Enter the desired style of poem: ")

subject = input("Enter the subject of the poem: ")

user_instructions = input("Enter any additional instructions: ")

# Generate the dynamic prompt

prompt = prompt_template.format(
    style=style, subject=subject, user_instructions=user_instructions
)

# Initialize the LLM

llm = OpenAI(temperature=0.8)
```

```
# Get the poem from the LLM

poem = llm(prompt)

print(poem)
```

In this example, the prompt changes based on the user's input for the style, subject, and additional instructions.

Real-World Examples

- Personalized Chatbots: A chatbot that remembers your previous interactions and tailors its responses accordingly.
- Interactive Storytelling: A story-generating application where the user's choices influence the plot and characters.
- Adaptive Educational Tools: An educational tool that adjusts the difficulty level and content based on the student's progress.

Benefits of Dynamic Prompts

- Personalization: Tailor the LLM's output to individual users or specific contexts.
- Engagement: Create more interactive and engaging experiences.
- Adaptability: Adjust the LLM's behavior based on real-time feedback or changing circumstances.

Improving LLM Output Quality

You're right to focus on quality! It's not just about getting an LLM to respond; it's about getting a *good* response. Let's explore some techniques to refine the output and make it even better.

Why Output Quality Matters

The quality of an LLM's output is crucial for several reasons:

- Accuracy and Reliability: Inaccurate or unreliable outputs can lead to misinformation, poor decision-making, and even harmful consequences.
- User Experience: High-quality outputs are essential for creating a positive user experience, whether it's in a chatbot, a writing assistant, or any other LLM-powered application.
- Trust and Confidence: Users are more likely to trust and engage with LLMs that consistently produce high-quality outputs.

Techniques for Improving Output Quality

Here are some key techniques you can use to enhance the quality of LLM outputs:

1. Parameter Tuning

LLMs have various parameters that can be adjusted to influence their behavior. Two important parameters for controlling output quality are:

- Temperature: This parameter controls the randomness of the LLM's output.

    Lower temperature (e.g., 0.1): More deterministic and focused outputs, often good for factual or informative tasks.

    Higher temperature (e.g., 0.8): More creative and unpredictable outputs, suitable for creative writing or brainstorming.

- Top-k Sampling: This technique limits the LLM's choices to the top k most likely words at each step during text generation. This can improve the coherence and quality of the generated text by preventing the model from selecting unlikely or nonsensical words.

Code Example (Python with LangChain)

```python
from langchain.llms import OpenAI

# Initialize the LLM with a lower temperature for more focused output

llm = OpenAI(temperature=0.2)

# Generate text from the LLM

text = llm("Explain the theory of relativity in simple terms.")

print(text)
```

2. Prompt Engineering Techniques

We've already discussed many prompt engineering techniques that can improve output quality, including:

- Clarity, Specificity, and Context: Providing clear instructions, specific details, and relevant context helps the LLM understand your intent and generate more accurate and relevant responses.
- Prompt Variations: Experimenting with different prompt variations can help you find the prompt that elicits the best output from the LLM.
- Dynamic Prompts: Using dynamic prompts to incorporate user feedback or adjust the LLM's behavior based on previous interactions can lead to more relevant and personalized outputs.

3. Output Filtering and Post-Processing

You can further improve output quality by filtering or post-processing the LLM's output. This might involve:

- Removing Irrelevant Content: Filtering out any parts of the output that are not relevant to the task or user query.
- Correcting Errors: Identifying and correcting any factual errors, grammatical mistakes, or inconsistencies in the output.
- Reformatting: Reformatting the output to improve its readability or presentation (e.g., adding headings, bullet points, or tables).

4. Fine-tuning

Fine-tuning is a more advanced technique that involves training the LLM on a smaller, task-specific dataset to improve its performance on that particular task. This can be particularly useful for tasks that require specialized knowledge or a specific writing style.

Real-World Examples

- Content Creation: A marketing team uses parameter tuning and prompt engineering to generate high-quality product descriptions that are informative, engaging, and free of errors.
- Chatbots: A customer support team uses output filtering and post-processing to ensure that the chatbot's responses are accurate, helpful, and consistent with the company's brand voice.
- Code Generation: A software developer uses fine-tuning to train an LLM to generate code that adheres to specific coding standards and best practices.

By combining these techniques, you can significantly improve the quality of LLM outputs and build applications that are more accurate, reliable, and user-friendly. Remember that improving output quality is an ongoing process that requires continuous evaluation, experimentation, and refinement.

Hallucinations

In the context of LLMs, hallucinations refer to the generation of incorrect or nonsensical information that is not supported by the input or any real-world knowledge. It's like the LLM is making things up, often in a very convincing way.

Why do hallucinations occur?

- Limited Knowledge: LLMs are trained on vast amounts of data, but their knowledge is still limited. When faced with a question or prompt that goes beyond their knowledge, they may try to fill in the gaps with fabricated information.
- Statistical Patterns: LLMs learn to generate text by identifying statistical patterns in the data they are trained on. Sometimes, these patterns can lead them to generate plausible-sounding but ultimately incorrect outputs.
- Lack of Grounding: LLMs don't have a true understanding of the real world. They lack the common sense and contextual awareness that humans have, which can lead to factual errors.

Dealing with Hallucinations

Here are some strategies to mitigate hallucinations:

Prompt Engineering:

- Provide Context: Give the LLM as much relevant context as possible to help it ground its responses in reality.
- Ask for Sources: Encourage the LLM to provide sources or evidence for its claims.
- Constrain the Output: Limit the LLM's freedom to generate text by providing specific constraints or guidelines.

External Verification:

- Fact-Checking: Use external sources or tools to verify the accuracy of the LLM's output.

- Human Review: Have human reviewers check the LLM's output for factual errors or inconsistencies.

Model Training:

- Improve Training Data: Train LLMs on more diverse and comprehensive datasets to reduce knowledge gaps.
- Reinforcement Learning: Use reinforcement learning techniques to train LLMs to distinguish between correct and incorrect information.

Bias

Bias in LLMs refers to the tendency of the model to generate outputs that reflect biases present in its training data. This can lead to outputs that are discriminatory, offensive, or perpetuate harmful stereotypes.

Why does bias occur?

- Biased Training Data: LLMs learn from the data they are trained on. If the training data contains biases, the LLM will likely inherit those biases.
- Lack of Diversity: If the training data is not diverse and representative of different perspectives and experiences, the LLM may develop a skewed view of the world.

Dealing with Bias

Here are some strategies to mitigate bias:

Data Curation:

- **Diverse and Representative Data:** Use training data that is diverse and representative of different demographics, cultures, and viewpoints.
- **Bias Detection and Mitigation:** Develop tools and techniques to detect and mitigate bias in training data.

Prompt Engineering:

Neutral Prompts: Use prompts that are neutral and avoid leading the LLM toward biased responses.

Explicitly Address Bias: Include instructions in the prompt that encourage the LLM to generate fair and unbiased outputs.

Model Training:

- Fine-tuning: Fine-tune LLMs on datasets that promote fairness and inclusivity.
- Adversarial Training: Use adversarial training techniques to make the LLM more robust to biased inputs.

Evaluation and Monitoring:

- Bias Metrics: Develop metrics to evaluate the bias in LLM outputs.
- Ongoing Monitoring: Continuously monitor LLM outputs for bias and take corrective action as needed.

Real-World Examples

- Content Moderation: Social media platforms use LLMs to detect and remove harmful or biased content.
- News Generation: News organizations use LLMs to generate news articles, but they need to be vigilant about potential bias in the outputs.
- Customer Service: Companies use LLMs for customer service, but they need to ensure that the LLMs treat all customers fairly and respectfully.

Ethical Considerations

Dealing with hallucinations and bias in LLMs is not just a technical challenge; it also raises important ethical considerations. It's crucial to use LLMs responsibly and to be mindful of their potential impact on individuals and society.

Chapter 3: LLM Chains: Building Sequential Workflows

LLM chains are where you start to see the real power of LangChain and how you can orchestrate LLMs to accomplish complex tasks. It's like building a sophisticated assembly line where each LLM (or other tool) plays a specific role.

3.1 Introduction to LLM Chains

In the previous chapters, we explored how to use LLMs for individual tasks, such as generating text, answering questions, or summarizing articles. But what if you want to accomplish something more complex? What if you want to analyze a document, extract key information, translate it into another language, and then generate a report based on that information?

This is where LLM chains come in. An LLM chain is a sequence of steps that involve one or more LLMs, potentially combined with other tools or data sources. Each step in the chain performs a specific operation, and the output of one step becomes the input for the next.

Think of it like an assembly line:

1. Raw Materials: You start with some initial input, like a document or a user query.
2. Step 1: The first LLM (or tool) performs an operation on the input, like summarizing the document or identifying key entities.
3. Step 2: The output of the first step becomes the input for the second step, where another LLM might translate the summary or generate a response based on the extracted entities.

4. Final Product: The chain continues until the final output is produced, which could be a report, a translation, or any other desired result.

Why are LLM Chains Powerful?

LLM chains offer several advantages:

- Modular Design: Chains allow you to break down complex tasks into smaller, more manageable steps. This makes your code easier to understand, maintain, and debug.
- Flexibility: You can easily combine different LLMs, prompts, and tools in a chain to create custom workflows tailored to your specific needs. You're not limited to a single LLM or a single type of task.
- Reusability: You can reuse chains or individual chain components across different projects, saving time and effort. This promotes a more efficient development process.
- Increased Capabilities: Chains enable you to build more sophisticated applications that can perform a wider range of tasks. You can essentially orchestrate LLMs to accomplish complex goals that would be difficult or impossible with a single LLM.

Real-World Examples

Here are some examples of how LLM chains can be used in real-world applications:

- Automated Content Creation: A marketing team uses an LLM chain to generate social media posts. The chain starts by summarizing a blog post, then extracts key quotes, and finally generates engaging social media captions with relevant hashtags.
- Complex Question Answering: A research assistant uses an LLM chain to answer complex questions that require information from multiple sources. The chain first searches a database of research papers, then summarizes the relevant

papers, and finally synthesizes the information to answer the question.
- Code Generation and Debugging: A software developer uses an LLM chain to generate code and then debug it. The first LLM in the chain generates code based on a natural language description. The second LLM analyzes the code and suggests improvements or identifies potential errors.

Key Concepts in LLM Chains

- Input and Output: Each step in a chain takes some input and produces some output. The output of one step becomes the input for the next.
- LLMs and Tools: Chains can include LLMs, other tools (like Python functions or external APIs), or a combination of both.
- Prompts: Prompts are used to guide the LLMs at each step of the chain, ensuring they perform the desired actions.

By understanding the basic concepts of LLM chains, you can start to see the vast potential they offer for building powerful and versatile LLM applications. In the next sections, we'll explore the different types of chains and how to build them using LangChain.

3.2 Types of Chains

LangChain provides several types of chains, each designed for different purposes:

Sequential Chains

A sequential chain, as the name suggests, executes a series of steps in a specific order. The output of one step becomes the input for the next, creating a linear flow of information and actions.

Think of it like a recipe:

1. Step 1: Gather your ingredients (the initial input).

2. Step 2: Perform the first action, like chopping vegetables (the first LLM or tool).
3. Step 3: Use the result of the first step (chopped vegetables) to perform the next action, like sautéing them (the second LLM or tool).
4. Continue: Keep following the steps in order until you reach the final dish (the final output).

Key Characteristics of Sequential Chains

- Order: The steps in a sequential chain are executed in a predefined order. This order is crucial to the chain's functionality, as each step relies on the output of the previous step.
- Linearity: The flow of information is linear, moving from one step to the next without any branching or decision-making.
- Simplicity: Sequential chains are relatively simple to understand and implement, making them a good starting point for building LLM workflows.

Building Sequential Chains with LangChain

LangChain provides a convenient way to create sequential chains using the SequentialChain class.

Code Example (Python with LangChain)

```
Python

from langchain.chains import LLMChain, SequentialChain

from langchain.llms import OpenAI

from langchain.prompts import PromptTemplate[1]

# Define the prompt templates
```

```
template1 = """
You are a helpful assistant that summarizes news
articles.

Summarize the following article:

{article_text}
"""

prompt_template1 =
PromptTemplate(input_variables=["article_text"],
template=template1)

template2 = """
You are a helpful assistant that translates text
into Spanish.

Translate the following summary into Spanish:

{summary}
"""

prompt_template2 =
PromptTemplate(input_variables=["summary"],
template=template2)

# Initialize the LLMs

llm1 = OpenAI(temperature=0)

llm2 = OpenAI(temperature=0)

# Create the LLM chains
```

```
chain1 = LLMChain(llm=llm1,
prompt=prompt_template1)

chain2 = LLMChain(llm=llm2,
prompt=prompt_template2)

# Create the sequential chain
overall_chain = SequentialChain(
    chains=[chain1, chain2],
    input_variables=["article_text"],
    output_variables=["spanish_translation"],
)

# Run the sequential chain
article_text = "This is a news article about the latest developments in artificial intelligence..."

spanish_translation = overall_chain.run(article_text)

print(spanish_translation)
```

In this example, we create a sequential chain that first summarizes a news article and then translates the summary into Spanish. The SequentialChain class takes a list of chains as input and executes them in order.

Real-World Examples

- Document Processing: A company uses a sequential chain to process legal documents. The chain first extracts key clauses from the document, then summarizes those clauses,

and finally generates a report highlighting potential risks and obligations.
- Data Analysis: A data analyst uses a sequential chain to analyze customer feedback. The chain first classifies the feedback as positive, negative, or neutral, then extracts key themes and topics, and finally generates a report with actionable insights.
- Automated Writing: A writer uses a sequential chain to generate different creative text formats. The chain first generates a story idea, then writes a short story based on that idea, and finally creates a poem inspired by the story.

Benefits of Sequential Chains

- Clear Structure: Sequential chains provide a clear and logical structure for complex workflows.
- Ease of Implementation: They are relatively easy to implement and understand, even for beginners.
- Versatility: They can be used for a wide range of tasks, from simple to complex.

Router Chains

Router chains, unlike sequential chains, don't follow a fixed, linear path. Instead, they dynamically determine which step to execute next based on certain conditions or rules. This allows you to create more flexible and intelligent workflows that can handle a variety of inputs and situations.

How Router Chains Work

A router chain typically involves:

1. Initial Step: An initial step, often involving an LLM, analyzes the input (e.g., a user query, a document) to determine its characteristics or intent.

2. **Routing Logic:** Based on the analysis, the chain applies a set of rules or conditions to decide which subsequent step to execute. This routing logic can be implemented using simple if-else statements or more complex decision-making algorithms.
3. **Destination Chains:** The router chain directs the input to one of several possible "destination chains," each designed to handle a specific type of input or task.

Example:

Let's say you're building a customer service chatbot. You could use a router chain to handle different types of customer queries:

1. **Initial Step:** An LLM analyzes the customer's message to determine the intent (e.g., product information, order status, technical support).
2. **Routing Logic:** Based on the intent, the router chain directs the message to the appropriate destination chain:

    Product Information Chain: Provides details about products, features, and pricing.

    Order Status Chain: Checks the status of an order and provides updates.

    Technical Support Chain: Troubleshoots technical issues and provides solutions.

Building Router Chains with LangChain

LangChain provides tools for building router chains, although the specific implementation can vary depending on the complexity of your routing logic. You might use conditional statements, custom functions, or even separate LLMs to determine the routing.

Simplified Code Example (Conceptual)

```python
# This is a simplified conceptual example, not actual LangChain code

def route_query(query):
    # Analyze the query (e.g., using an LLM)
    intent = analyze_intent(query)
    # Route based on intent
    if intent == "product_info":
        return product_info_chain.run(query)
    elif intent == "order_status":
        return order_status_chain.run(query)
    else:
        return general_support_chain.run(query)

# ... (define the product_info_chain, order_status_chain, etc.)

# Run the router chain
user_query = "What is the price of the latest smartphone?"
response = route_query(user_query)
print(response)
```

Real-World Examples

- Personalized Recommendations: An e-commerce website uses a router chain to provide personalized product recommendations based on user preferences and browsing history.
- Adaptive Educational Tools: An educational platform uses a router chain to adapt the learning path and content based on the student's skill level and learning style.
- Multi-lingual Support: A customer service chatbot uses a router chain to direct queries to different LLMs specialized in different languages.

Benefits of Router Chains

- Flexibility: Handle a variety of inputs and situations dynamically.
- Efficiency: Direct queries to the most appropriate LLM or tool, optimizing resource usage.
- Personalization: Provide tailored experiences based on user needs and preferences.

Transform Chains

Transform chains, as the name implies, modify or transform the output of one step before passing it to the next. This transformation can involve various operations, such as:

- Data Cleaning: Removing irrelevant information, correcting errors, or standardizing formats.
- Data Conversion: Converting data from one format to another (e.g., text to JSON, list to dictionary).
- Data Enrichment: Adding additional information or context to the data.
- Text Manipulation: Modifying the text, such as changing the case, replacing words, or extracting specific elements.

Why Use Transform Chains?

- Data Preparation: LLMs often require data in a specific format or structure. Transform chains ensure that the data is properly prepared before being passed to the next step in the workflow.
- Improved Accuracy: By cleaning and refining the data, transform chains can improve the accuracy and reliability of subsequent LLM outputs.
- Enhanced Flexibility: Transform chains allow you to integrate LLMs with other tools and processes that may require different data formats or structures.
- Customization: You can create custom transformation functions to tailor the data to your specific needs.

Building Transform Chains with LangChain

While LangChain doesn't have a dedicated TransformChain class, you can easily build transform chains by combining LLMs with other tools or functions.

Code Example (Python with LangChain)

Python

```
from langchain.chains import LLMChain

from langchain.llms import OpenAI

from langchain.prompts import PromptTemplate[1]

# Define the prompt template

template = """

You are a helpful assistant that generates lists of items.

Generate a list of {number} {category}.

"""
```

```python
prompt_template = PromptTemplate(
    input_variables=["number", "category"],
    template=template,
)
# Initialize the LLM
llm = OpenAI(temperature=0)
# Create the LLM chain
chain = LLMChain(llm=llm, prompt=prompt_template)
# Define a transformation function
def transform_output(text):
    """Converts a list of items into a JSON format."""
    import json
    items = text.strip().split("\n")
    return json.dumps(items)
# Run the chain and transform the output
output = chain.run({"number": 5, "category": "fruits"})
transformed_output = transform_output(output)
print(transformed_output)
```

In this example, we create an LLM chain that generates a list of fruits. We then define a transform_output function that converts the list into a JSON format.

Real-World Examples

- Data Extraction and Analysis: A company uses a transform chain to extract data from invoices. The chain first uses an LLM to identify the relevant information in the invoice (e.g., invoice number, date, amount). Then, a transformation function extracts those values and stores them in a structured format (e.g., a dictionary or a database).
- Chatbot Interactions: A chatbot uses a transform chain to format user messages before passing them to the LLM. The chain might remove unnecessary characters, correct spelling errors, or translate the message into a different language.
- Code Generation: A developer uses a transform chain to generate code in a specific format. The chain first uses an LLM to generate the code logic. Then, a transformation function formats the code according to specific style guidelines or adds comments and documentation.

Benefits of Transform Chains

- Data Quality: Transform chains help ensure that data is clean, consistent, and properly formatted for subsequent processing.
- Integration: They enable seamless integration of LLMs with other tools and processes.
- Customization: You can create custom transformation functions to meet your specific needs.

3.3 Building Chains with LangChain

LangChain makes it surprisingly easy to construct these powerful chains. Let's explore the tools and techniques for building chains that can tackle a wide range of tasks.

The Building Blocks of Chains

Before we start building, let's recap the key components that make up LLM chains:

- LLMs: These are the core engines of your chains, providing the language understanding and generation capabilities. LangChain supports a variety of LLMs, including OpenAI models, Hugging Face models, and more.
- Prompts: Prompts guide the LLMs at each step, providing instructions and context. LangChain's PromptTemplate class helps you create and manage prompts effectively.
- Chains: Chains link together LLMs and other components in a specific order or based on certain conditions. LangChain offers different chain types, such as sequential, router, and transform chains.
- Other Tools: You can include other tools in your chains, such as Python functions, external APIs, or data loaders. This allows you to integrate LLMs with a wide range of functionalities.

Constructing Chains with LangChain

LangChain provides a simple and intuitive API for constructing chains. Here's a breakdown of the general process:

1. Initialize LLMs: Choose the LLMs you want to use and initialize them with any necessary parameters (e.g., temperature, API keys).
2. Create Prompts: Define the prompts that will guide the LLMs at each step. Use PromptTemplate to create reusable templates with variables.

3. Define Chain Components: Create the individual components of your chain, which could be LLMChain instances, Python functions, or other tools.
4. Assemble the Chain: Use the appropriate chain class (e.g., SequentialChain, LLMRouterChain) to assemble the components into a complete chain.
5. Run the Chain: Execute the chain by providing the initial input and retrieving the final output.

Code Example (Python with LangChain)

```python
from langchain.chains import LLMChain, SequentialChain

from langchain.llms import OpenAI

from langchain.prompts import PromptTemplate[1]

# Initialize the LLM

llm = OpenAI(temperature=0)

# Define the prompt templates

summary_template = """
You are a helpful assistant that summarizes text.

Summarize the following text:

{text}
"""

summary_prompt = PromptTemplate(input_variables=["text"], template=summary_template)
```

```python
qa_template = """

You are a helpful assistant that answers questions about summaries.

Answer the following question based on the provided summary:

Summary: {summary}

Question: {question}
"""

qa_prompt = PromptTemplate(
    input_variables=["summary", "question"],
    template=qa_template
)

# Create the LLM chains
summary_chain = LLMChain(llm=llm, prompt=summary_prompt)

qa_chain = LLMChain(llm=llm, prompt=qa_prompt)

# Create the sequential chain
overall_chain = SequentialChain(
    chains=[summary_chain, qa_chain],
    input_variables=["text", "question"],
    output_variables=["answer"],
)
```

```
# Run the chain

text = "This is a long article about the history
of space exploration..."

question = "What were some of the key milestones
in early space exploration?"

answer = overall_chain.run({"text": text,
"question": question})

print(answer)
```

In this example, we build a sequential chain that first summarizes a text and then answers a question based on the summary.

Tips and Best Practices

- Start Simple: Begin with simple chains and gradually add complexity as needed.
- Use Meaningful Names: Give your chains and components meaningful names to improve code readability.
- Test Each Component: Test each component of your chain individually to ensure it's working correctly before assembling the complete chain.
- Document Your Code: Add comments and documentation to your code to explain the purpose and functionality of each chain and component.
- Experiment and Iterate: Don't be afraid to experiment with different chain configurations and parameters to find the best solution for your task.

Real-World Examples

- Automated Report Generation: A financial analyst uses LangChain to build a chain that automatically generates reports from financial data. The chain extracts key metrics

from the data, summarizes trends, and generates a report with visualizations.
- **Personalized Learning:** An educational platform uses LangChain to create personalized learning paths for students. The chain assesses the student's knowledge, recommends relevant content, and provides feedback on their progress.
- **Creative Content Generation:** A marketing agency uses LangChain to build a chain that generates creative content for different platforms. The chain starts with a concept or idea, generates text variations, and adapts the content for different social media platforms.

By mastering the art of building chains with LangChain, you can unlock the full potential of LLMs and create sophisticated applications that can automate tasks, analyze information, and generate creative outputs.

3.4 Practical Examples

Let's look at some practical examples of how LLM chains can be used:

Extracting Information from Text

You're focusing on a very practical application of LLM chains! Extracting information from text is a common need in many fields, and LLMs, combined with the power of chains, can automate this process effectively.

Text data often contains valuable information hidden within unstructured sentences and paragraphs. Manually extracting this information can be time-consuming, tedious, and error-prone, especially when dealing with large volumes of text.

How LLMs Can Help

LLMs excel at understanding and processing natural language. They can analyze text, identify key entities and relationships, and extract the information you need. By incorporating LLMs into chains, you can automate the information extraction process and make it more efficient and accurate.

Types of Information You Can Extract

- Key Entities: Names of people, organizations, locations, dates, products, etc.
- Relationships: Connections between entities, such as "X is the CEO of Y" or "A is located in B."
- Keywords and Topics: The main subjects or themes discussed in the text.
- Sentiment: The overall sentiment expressed in the text (e.g., positive, negative, neutral).
- Specific Facts or Details: Answers to specific questions about the text.

Building Chains for Information Extraction

Here's a common approach to building chains for information extraction:

1. Text Preprocessing: If necessary, preprocess the text to clean it up and prepare it for the LLM. This might involve removing irrelevant characters, correcting spelling errors, or splitting the text into smaller chunks.
2. LLM for Understanding: Use an LLM to analyze the text and identify the relevant information. This might involve asking the LLM specific questions or prompting it to extract entities or relationships.
3. Transformation (Optional): If needed, use a transformation function to convert the LLM's output into a structured format, such as a dictionary, a list, or a JSON object. This makes it easier to store and process the extracted information.

Code Example (Python with LangChain)

```python
from langchain.chains import LLMChain

from langchain.llms import OpenAI

from langchain.prompts import PromptTemplate

# Initialize the LLM

llm = OpenAI(temperature=0)

# Define the prompt template

template = """
You are a helpful assistant that extracts information from text.

Extract the following information from the text below:

* Names of people

* Names of organizations

* Locations mentioned

Text: {text}

Extracted Information:
"""

prompt_template = PromptTemplate(input_variables=["text"], template=template)
```

```python
# Create the LLM chain

chain = LLMChain(llm=llm, prompt=prompt_template)

# Run the chain

text = "John Doe, the CEO of Acme Corporation, announced today that the company will open a new office in London."

extracted_info = chain.run(text)

print(extracted_info)
```

Real-World Examples

- Resume Parsing: HR departments use LLM chains to extract key information from resumes, such as skills, experience, and education.
- Contract Analysis: Legal teams use LLM chains to extract important clauses and obligations from contracts.
- Social Media Monitoring: Companies use LLM chains to extract sentiment and key topics from social media posts.
- News Aggregation: News aggregators use LLM chains to extract key events and entities from news articles.

Benefits of Using LLMs for Information Extraction

- Automation: Automates the process of extracting information from text, saving time and effort.
- Accuracy: LLMs can accurately identify and extract information, reducing errors.
- Scalability: LLMs can handle large volumes of text data efficiently.
- Adaptability: LLMs can be adapted to extract different types of information from various text formats.

Generating Different Creative Text Formats

Generating creative text formats is where these models can truly showcase their ability to mimic human imagination and produce engaging content.

While LLMs can generate various types of text, creative writing takes it a step further. It's about producing content that is not just informative or functional but also imaginative, engaging, and potentially even artistic.

Types of Creative Text Formats LLMs Can Generate

- Stories: Short stories, novels, scripts for plays or movies, even interactive narratives where the user's choices influence the plot.
- Poetry: Various forms of poetry, including sonnets, haikus, free verse, and more. LLMs can even be guided to adopt specific poetic styles or rhyme schemes.
- Dialogue: Conversations between characters, whether for fictional stories, games, or chatbots.
- Musical Pieces: Lyrics for songs, potentially even melodies or musical notation.
- Other Creative Content: Letters, emails, social media posts, marketing copy, and more.

Building Chains for Creative Text Generation

Here's how you can use chains to generate different creative text formats:

1. Seed Generation (Optional): Start with an LLM chain that generates a creative seed or starting point. This could be a story idea, a character description, a setting, or a theme.
2. Format-Specific Chain: Create separate chains for each creative text format you want to generate. These chains should use prompts tailored to the specific format (e.g., a prompt for writing poems, a prompt for writing dialogue).

3. Iterative Refinement: Use the output of one chain as input for another to iteratively refine and expand upon the creative content. For example, you could generate a story idea, then use that idea to write a short story, then use the story to create a poem, and so on.

Code Example (Python with LangChain)

```python
from langchain.chains import LLMChain, SequentialChain

from langchain.llms import OpenAI

from langchain.prompts import PromptTemplate[1]

# Initialize the LLM

llm = OpenAI(temperature=0.8)   # Higher temperature for creativity

# Define the prompt templates

story_template = """

You are a helpful assistant that writes fantasy stories.

Write a short fantasy story about {story_idea}.

"""

story_prompt = PromptTemplate(input_variables=["story_idea"], template=story_template)

poem_template = """
```

```
You are a helpful assistant that writes poems
based on stories.

Write a poem inspired by the following story:

{story}
"""

poem_prompt =
PromptTemplate(input_variables=["story"],
template=poem_template)

# Create the LLM chains

story_chain = LLMChain(llm=llm,
prompt=story_prompt)

poem_chain = LLMChain(llm=llm,
prompt=poem_prompt)

# Create the sequential chain

overall_chain = SequentialChain(

    chains=[story_chain, poem_chain],

    input_variables=["story_idea"],

    output_variables=["poem"],

)

# Run the chain

story_idea = "a young witch who discovers a
hidden world"

poem = overall_chain.run(story_idea)
```

```
print(poem)
```

Real-World Examples

- Interactive Storytelling: A game developer uses LLM chains to generate dynamic dialogue and branching narratives for a role-playing game.
- Marketing Campaigns: A marketing team uses LLM chains to generate creative slogans, taglines, and social media content for a new product launch.
- Personalized Content: A content creation platform uses LLM chains to generate personalized stories, poems, or songs based on user preferences.

Benefits of Using LLMs for Creative Text Generation

- Enhanced Creativity: LLMs can help overcome writer's block and generate new ideas.
- Increased Productivity: LLMs can quickly generate different creative text formats, saving time and effort.
- Exploration of Styles: LLMs can be used to explore different writing styles and genres.
- Personalization: LLMs can generate creative content tailored to specific audiences or individuals.

By incorporating LLMs into your creative process, you can unlock new possibilities for storytelling, poetry, and other forms of artistic expression.

Chapter 4: Agents and Autonomous Interactions

Agents take LLMs to the next level, enabling them to interact with the world, make decisions, and achieve goals. It's like giving your LLMs a sense of agency and purpose.

4.1 Rise of LLM Agents

LLM agents represent a significant leap forward in artificial intelligence, moving beyond simple input-output interactions towards more autonomous and intelligent behavior.

In the earlier chapters, we explored how LLMs can perform various tasks, such as generating text, translating languages, and answering questions. However, these LLMs primarily acted as passive responders, reacting to prompts and providing outputs without much agency or decision-making capability.

LLM agents, on the other hand, are designed to be more active and autonomous. They can interact with their environment, make decisions, and take actions to achieve specific goals. This shift from passive responders to active agents opens up a whole new world of possibilities for LLM applications.

What Makes an LLM an Agent?

An LLM agent is characterized by its ability to:

- Perceive: Gather information from its surroundings. This could involve processing text, analyzing data, or even interacting with the real world through sensors or APIs.
- Reason: Use its knowledge and understanding to make sense of the information it perceives and to plan its actions.

- Act: Take actions that affect its environment. This could involve generating text, manipulating data, or controlling physical devices.
- Learn: Update its knowledge and behavior based on the outcomes of its actions, allowing it to adapt to new situations and improve its performance over time.

Why are LLM Agents Gaining Prominence?

Several factors contribute to the rising importance of LLM agents:

- Increased Complexity of Tasks: As we seek to automate more complex and sophisticated tasks, we need LLMs that can go beyond simple input-output interactions and exhibit more autonomous behavior.
- Need for Adaptability: Many real-world applications require LLMs to adapt to changing circumstances and make decisions in dynamic environments. Agents provide the flexibility and adaptability needed for such applications.
- Desire for Automation: Agents can automate tasks that previously required human intervention, freeing up human time and resources for more creative or strategic endeavors.
- Advances in LLM Capabilities: Recent advances in LLM technology, such as improved reasoning and planning abilities, have made it possible to develop more capable and sophisticated agents.

Real-World Examples of LLM Agents

- Customer Service: Imagine a customer service agent that can not only answer questions but also proactively resolve issues by interacting with various systems, such as checking order status, processing refunds, or scheduling appointments.
- Data Analysis: An LLM agent could analyze large datasets, identify trends, generate reports, and even make predictions or recommendations based on the data.

- Content Creation: An LLM agent could generate creative content, such as stories, poems, or articles, while also taking into account user feedback and preferences to personalize the output.
- Robotics: LLM agents could control robots in complex environments, allowing them to navigate, interact with objects, and perform tasks autonomously.

Key Benefits of LLM Agents

- Automation: Automate complex, multi-step tasks that previously required human intervention.
- Problem-solving: Solve problems that require reasoning, planning, and decision-making in dynamic environments.
- Personalization: Provide tailored experiences by adapting to individual user needs and preferences.
- Efficiency: Optimize workflows and processes by automating repetitive tasks and making intelligent decisions.

As LLM technology continues to evolve, we can expect to see even more sophisticated and capable agents emerge, transforming the way we interact with computers and automate tasks.

4.2 Agent Architectures and Use Cases

There are various architectures for designing LLM agents. Let's look at two common ones:

ReAct Agents

ReAct, which stands for **Reasoning and Acting**, is an agent architecture designed to enable LLMs to perform tasks that require a continuous loop of thinking and doing. It's like a detective solving a case: they gather clues (observe), think about the clues (reason), and take actions to gather more clues or solve the case (act).

The ReAct Loop

ReAct agents operate in a cycle of three main steps:

1. Thought: The agent uses an LLM to reason about the current situation. This involves analyzing available information, considering its goals, and generating potential actions. This "thought" process is often expressed in natural language, allowing us to understand the agent's reasoning.
2. Action: The agent selects an action from the generated options. This action could be anything from retrieving information from a database to interacting with a user or controlling a physical device.
3. Observation: The agent observes the result of its action. This observation provides feedback that informs the next "thought" process, allowing the agent to learn and adapt its behavior.

Key Features of ReAct Agents

- Dynamic Decision-Making: ReAct agents can dynamically adapt their actions based on the changing environment and the outcomes of previous actions.
- Explainability: The "thought" process of ReAct agents is often expressed in natural language, making it easier to understand the agent's reasoning and decision-making.
- Versatility: ReAct agents can be applied to a wide range of tasks that involve both reasoning and action.

Building ReAct Agents with LangChain

LangChain provides tools and components to simplify the development of ReAct agents.

- AgentExecutor: This class manages the ReAct loop, handling the interaction between the LLM, the tools, and the environment.

- Toolkits: LangChain offers toolkits that provide pre-built tools for common tasks, such as web browsing, calculation, or Python REPL interaction.

Code Example (Python with LangChain)

```Python
from langchain.agents import load_tools
from langchain.agents import initialize_agent
from langchain.agents import AgentType
from langchain.llms import OpenAI

# Load the Python REPL tool
tools = load_tools(["python_repl"], llm=OpenAI(temperature=0))

# Initialize the ReAct agent
agent = initialize_agent(
    tools,
    OpenAI(temperature=0),
    agent=AgentType.ZERO_SHOT_REACT_DESCRIPTION,
    verbose=True,
)

# Run the agent
task = "Calculate the factorial of 5."
result = agent.run(task)
```

```
print(result)
```

In this example, we use the python_repl tool to allow the agent to execute Python code. The agent uses the LLM to understand the task, decides to use the Python REPL tool to calculate the factorial, and returns the result.

Real-World Examples

- Automated Data Analysis: A ReAct agent can analyze data by iteratively querying a database, visualizing the results, and generating reports.
- Interactive Storytelling: A ReAct agent can create interactive stories where the user's choices influence the plot and the agent dynamically generates the next part of the story.
- Task Automation: A ReAct agent can automate tasks that involve interacting with different software applications or websites, such as booking a flight, ordering food, or managing a calendar.

Benefits of ReAct Agents

- Adaptability: ReAct agents can adapt to dynamic environments and changing circumstances.
- Explainability: Their reasoning process is often transparent, making it easier to understand their decisions.
- Efficiency: They can automate complex tasks that involve both reasoning and action.

Plan-and-Execute Agents

Plan-and-execute agents are designed for tasks that require more deliberation and foresight than the immediate reaction of ReAct agents. They excel in situations where a well-thought-out plan is crucial for success.

The Two-Phase Approach

As the name suggests, plan-and-execute agents operate in two distinct phases:

1. Planning Phase: The agent uses its knowledge and reasoning abilities to create a plan of action. This plan outlines the steps needed to achieve a specific goal, taking into account potential obstacles, constraints, and desired outcomes. This phase often involves breaking down a complex goal into smaller, more manageable sub-goals.
2. Execution Phase: Once the plan is formulated, the agent systematically executes the steps outlined in the plan. It monitors its progress, adjusts the plan as needed based on new information or unexpected events, and continues executing until the goal is achieved.

Key Features of Plan-and-Execute Agents

- Strategic Thinking: These agents excel at tasks that require strategic thinking, long-term planning, and anticipation of future consequences.
- Goal-Oriented: They are highly goal-oriented, focusing on achieving a specific objective through a well-defined plan.
- Adaptability: While they follow a plan, they can adapt and adjust their actions based on new information or changes in the environment.
- Complex Task Handling: They are well-suited for handling complex tasks that involve multiple steps, dependencies, and potential obstacles.

Building Plan-and-Execute Agents with LangChain

LangChain provides tools and components that can be used to build plan-and-execute agents, although the specific implementation will depend on the complexity of the task and the planning strategy.

- LLMs for Planning: You can use LLMs to generate plans by providing prompts that describe the goal, constraints, and available actions.
- Chains for Execution: You can use chains to execute the steps in the plan, potentially incorporating other tools or LLMs for specific actions.
- Memory: Memory components can help the agent remember the plan, track its progress, and make adjustments as needed.

Simplified Code Example (Conceptual)

Python

```python
# This is a simplified conceptual example, not actual LangChain code

def generate_plan(goal, constraints):
    # Use an LLM to generate a plan
    prompt = f"Generate a plan to achieve the following goal: {goal}, considering these constraints: {constraints}"
    plan = llm(prompt)
    return plan

def execute_plan(plan):
    # Execute the steps in the plan
    for step in plan:
        # ... (code to execute the step)
# ... (define the goal and constraints)
```

```
# Generate the plan

plan = generate_plan(goal, constraints)

# Execute the plan

execute_plan(plan)
```

Real-World Examples

- Robotics: A plan-and-execute agent could control a robot in a warehouse, planning a path to retrieve items, avoiding obstacles, and adapting to changes in the environment.
- Game AI: A game AI agent could use a plan-and-execute approach to play strategy games, planning its moves, anticipating the opponent's actions, and adapting its strategy as needed.
- Project Management: An LLM agent could assist in project management by generating plans, assigning tasks, tracking progress, and adjusting deadlines based on real-time feedback.

Benefits of Plan-and-Execute Agents

- Strategic Decision-Making: These agents excel at strategic thinking and planning for complex tasks.
- Goal-Oriented Behavior: They are focused on achieving specific goals through well-defined plans.
- Adaptability: They can adjust their plans based on new information or unexpected events.

By understanding the plan-and-execute architecture and leveraging LangChain's tools, you can build intelligent agents that can tackle complex tasks, automate workflows, and make strategic decisions in dynamic environments.

4.3 Building Agents with LangChain

LangChain provides tools and components to simplify the development of LLM agents.

Tools and Toolkits

In the context of LLM agents, tools are functionalities that allow the agent to perform actions or access information beyond its core language processing abilities. These tools can be anything from simple Python functions to complex integrations with external APIs or databases.

Examples of Tools:

- Web Search: A tool that allows the agent to search the web and retrieve information from websites.
- Calculator: A tool that performs mathematical calculations.
- Python REPL: A tool that allows the agent to execute Python code and get the results.
- Database Access: A tool that allows the agent to query a database and retrieve data.
- API Interaction: A tool that interacts with external APIs, such as social media APIs, weather APIs, or payment gateways.

Why are Tools Important for LLM Agents?

Tools are crucial for LLM agents because they:

- Extend Capabilities: They expand the agent's capabilities beyond language processing, allowing it to interact with various data sources and perform actions in the real world.
- Enable Task Completion: They provide the necessary functionalities for the agent to complete complex tasks that require more than just language understanding.

- Promote Modularity: They allow you to build modular and reusable components that can be combined in different ways to create various agents.

LangChain Toolkits

LangChain provides **toolkits** that bundle together sets of tools for specific domains or tasks. This makes it easier to get started with building agents by providing pre-built tools and integrations.

Examples of LangChain Toolkits:

- google_search: Provides tools for searching the web using Google Search.
- python_repl: Provides tools for executing Python code.
- requests: Provides tools for interacting with web APIs using the requests library.
- terminal: Provides tools for executing commands in the operating system's terminal.

Code Example (Python with LangChain)

```python
Python

from langchain.agents import load_tools

from langchain.agents import initialize_agent

from langchain.agents import AgentType

from langchain.llms import OpenAI

# Load the Google Search and Python REPL tools

tools = load_tools(["google_search", "python_repl"], llm=OpenAI(temperature=0))

# Initialize the agent

agent = initialize_agent(
```

```
    tools,
    OpenAI(temperature=0),
    agent=AgentType.ZERO_SHOT_REACT_DESCRIPTION,
    verbose=True,
)
# Run the agent
task = "What is the capital of France? Calculate the square root of 16."
result = agent.run(task)
print(result)
```

In this example, we load the google_search and python_repl toolkits to equip the agent with web search and Python execution capabilities. The agent uses these tools to answer the questions and perform the calculation.

Real-World Examples

- Personal Assistant: A personal assistant agent might use tools for calendar management, email access, web browsing, and social media interaction to help users manage their daily tasks.
- Data Analyst Agent: A data analyst agent might use tools for database access, data visualization, and statistical analysis to extract insights from data and generate reports.
- E-commerce Agent: An e-commerce agent might use tools for product search, price comparison, and order placement to help users find and purchase products online.

Benefits of Using Tools and Toolkits

- Efficiency: Tools automate tasks and provide quick access to information, making agents more efficient.
- Versatility: Tools allow agents to perform a wider range of tasks and interact with various systems.
- Modularity: Toolkits promote modularity and reusability, making it easier to build and maintain agents.

Understanding the role of tools and toolkits and leveraging LangChain's resources, you can empower your LLM agents with the functionalities they need to interact with the world and accomplish a wide range of tasks.

4.4 Example: Building a Research Agent

Building a research agent is a great way to understand how LLMs can be combined with tools to perform complex tasks autonomously.

The Goal: Automating Research

Imagine having an AI assistant that can conduct research for you, sifting through vast amounts of information and summarizing the key findings. That's the power of a research agent.

Components of a Research Agent

A research agent typically needs the following capabilities:

- Information Retrieval: Access to information sources, such as the web, databases, or specific documents.
- Question Answering: Ability to understand research questions and extract relevant answers from the retrieved information.
- Summarization: Ability to condense information into concise summaries.

- Planning and Decision-Making: Ability to decide which sources to consult, which questions to ask, and how to synthesize the information.

Building a Research Agent with LangChain

LangChain provides the tools and framework to build such an agent. Here's a breakdown of the steps involved:

1. Choose Tools: Select the tools that your agent will need to access information. For web research, you can use the google_search toolkit. For accessing specific documents, you might use the text_splitter tool to break down large documents into smaller chunks.
2. Initialize the LLM: Choose an LLM and initialize it with the desired parameters.
3. Define the Agent: Use initialize_agent to create an agent. Specify the tools, the LLM, and the agent type (e.g., ZERO_SHOT_REACT_DESCRIPTION).
4. Run the Agent: Provide a research question to the agent and let it do its work.

Code Example (Python with LangChain)

```python
from langchain.agents import load_tools

from langchain.agents import initialize_agent

from langchain.agents import AgentType

from langchain.llms import OpenAI

# Load[1] the Google Search tool
tools = load_tools(["google_search"], llm=OpenAI(temperature=0))
```

```python
# Initialize the agent
agent = initialize_agent(
    tools,
    OpenAI(temperature=0),
    agent=AgentType.ZERO_SHOT_REACT_DESCRIPTION,
    verbose=True,
)

# Run the agent
question = "What are the latest advancements in solar energy technology?"
answer = agent.run(question)
print(answer)
```

In this example, the agent uses the Google Search tool to find information about advancements in solar energy technology. The verbose=True argument allows you to see the agent's thought process and actions.

Enhancing the Research Agent

You can further enhance the research agent by:

- Adding More Tools: Include tools for accessing other information sources, such as Wikipedia, news APIs, or research databases.
- Improving the Prompt: Refine the prompt to guide the agent towards more specific or comprehensive research.
- Incorporating Memory: Add memory to the agent so it can remember previous research and build upon its knowledge.

- Using a More Advanced Agent Type: Experiment with different agent types, such as ReAct or Plan-and-Execute, to see how they affect the research process.

Real-World Examples

- Academic Research: Researchers can use research agents to quickly gather and summarize information from various sources, accelerating the literature review process.
- Market Analysis: Businesses can use research agents to monitor market trends, competitor activities, and customer sentiment.
- Content Creation: Writers can use research agents to gather facts, statistics, and background information for their articles or stories.

Benefits of Research Agents

- Efficiency: Automate the research process, saving time and effort.
- Comprehensiveness: Access and synthesize information from multiple sources.
- Objectivity: Reduce potential bias by gathering information from diverse sources.
- Adaptability: Adapt to different research questions and information needs.

By building research agents with LangChain, you can harness the power of LLMs to automate information gathering and analysis, making research more efficient and insightful.

Chapter 5: Memory and Contextual Awareness

Memory is like giving your LLMs a sense of the past, allowing them to remember previous interactions and maintain context in conversations. This opens up a whole new dimension of possibilities.

5.1 Why Memory Matters for LLMs

Memory is like giving LLMs a history, a sense of the past, allowing them to remember previous interactions and maintain context in conversations. This is a game-changer for creating more human-like and personalized experiences.

The Limitations of Stateless LLMs

In their basic form, most LLMs operate in a stateless manner. This means that each interaction is treated as a brand new conversation, with no recollection of past exchanges. It's like encountering someone with amnesia every time you interact with them.

This statelessness can lead to several issues:

- Repetitive Responses: The LLM might repeat information or ask the same questions multiple times, as if it's encountering the user for the first time in every interaction.
- Inconsistent Behavior: The LLM might contradict itself or change its personality from one interaction to the next, lacking a coherent sense of self.
- Lack of Personalization: The LLM cannot tailor its responses based on the user's history, preferences, or past

interactions, leading to a generic and impersonal experience.

The Power of Memory

Adding memory to LLMs addresses these limitations and unlocks a whole new level of capability. It's like giving the LLM a memory bank where it can store and retrieve information about past interactions.

With memory, LLMs can:

- Maintain Context: Remember previous turns in a conversation, user preferences, and relevant information. This allows the LLM to understand the flow of the conversation and provide more coherent and meaningful responses.
- Personalize Interactions: Tailor responses based on the user's history and preferences. This creates a more engaging and personalized experience for the user.
- Exhibit Consistency: Maintain a consistent personality and avoid contradictions. This makes the LLM appear more reliable and trustworthy.
- Learn and Adapt: Learn from past interactions and improve their responses over time. This allows the LLM to become more knowledgeable and effective with each conversation.

Real-World Examples

Let's consider some real-world scenarios where memory is crucial for LLMs:

- Customer Service Chatbots: A chatbot with memory can remember customer details, past issues, and preferences, providing more personalized and efficient support.
- Personalized Learning Platforms: An educational platform with memory can track student progress, adapt the learning

path based on their strengths and weaknesses, and provide personalized feedback.
- Interactive Storytelling: A story-generating application with memory can remember user choices and previous events, creating dynamic and engaging narratives that evolve based on the user's interactions.

Technical Aspects of Memory

Memory in LLMs can be implemented in various ways. Some common approaches include:

- Storing Conversation History: Keeping a record of past messages or interactions.
- Summarizing Conversations: Generating concise summaries of past conversations to capture the essential information.
- Storing Entity Information: Remembering specific entities and their attributes, such as a user's name, preferences, or past purchases.

Benefits of Memory for LLMs

- Enhanced User Experience: Memory leads to more engaging, personalized, and human-like interactions.
- Improved Accuracy and Consistency: Memory helps LLMs maintain context and avoid contradictions, leading to more accurate and consistent responses.
- Increased Efficiency: Memory allows LLMs to learn from past interactions and improve their performance over time.

Understanding the importance of memory and how to incorporate it into your LLM applications, you can create more intelligent and interactive systems that can truly engage users and provide valuable services.

5.2 Memory Types in LangChain

LangChain provides different types of memory to suit various needs:

ConversationBufferMemory

Think of ConversationBufferMemory as a simple and direct approach to storing the history of a conversation. It's like keeping a detailed log of every message exchanged. ConversationBufferMemory essentially acts like a list. Every time there's an interaction in the conversation (a user message and the LLM's response), it adds those messages to the list. This creates a chronological record of the entire conversation.

When the LLM needs to generate a response, it can access this buffer and review the entire history of the conversation. This allows it to take previous messages into account, maintaining context and avoiding repetition.

Key Features

- Simplicity: This is a very simple and easy-to-understand memory type. It's essentially just a list of messages.
- Complete History: It stores the entire conversation history, providing full context to the LLM.
- Easy to Implement: It's straightforward to implement and use in LangChain.

Code Example (Python with LangChain)

```
Python

from langchain.chains import ConversationChain

from langchain.llms import OpenAI

from langchain.memory import ConversationBufferMemory[1]
```

```python
# Initialize the LLM and memory
llm = OpenAI(temperature=0)
memory = ConversationBufferMemory()

# Create the conversation chain with memory
conversation = ConversationChain(llm=llm, memory=memory, verbose=True)

# Start the conversation
conversation.predict(input="Hi, my name is Alice.")

conversation.predict(input="What was my name again?")
```

In this example, the ConversationBufferMemory stores the initial message where Alice introduces herself. When asked "What was my name again?", the LLM can access the memory buffer, find the previous message, and correctly respond with "Your name is Alice."

Limitations

While simple and effective for short conversations, ConversationBufferMemory has some limitations:

- Memory Size: As the conversation gets longer, the memory buffer can grow quite large, potentially impacting performance and efficiency.
- Lack of Summarization: It simply stores the raw conversation history without any summarization or analysis. This can make it less effective for very long conversations where the LLM might struggle to process the entire history.

Real-World Examples

Despite its limitations, ConversationBufferMemory can be useful in various scenarios:

- Short Conversations: For applications with relatively short conversations, such as simple chatbots or question-answering systems, this memory type can be sufficient.
- Debugging and Analysis: Storing the complete conversation history can be useful for debugging LLM applications and analyzing user interactions.
- Educational Applications: In educational settings, it can be helpful to review the complete history of a student's interaction with an LLM tutor.

If you're dealing with longer conversations or need more sophisticated memory management, you might consider other memory types offered by LangChain, such as ConversationSummaryMemory or EntityMemory. These provide more efficient ways to handle long conversations and store specific types of information.

ConversationSummaryMemory

ConversationSummaryMemory takes things a step further by condensing the conversation history into a concise summary. Think of it as a helpful assistant that keeps track of the main points of the conversation so the LLM doesn't have to remember every single detail.

Instead of storing the entire conversation verbatim like ConversationBufferMemory, ConversationSummaryMemory uses an LLM to create a summary of the conversation so far. This summary is then passed as context to the LLM in subsequent interactions, providing a condensed version of the conversation history.[1]

This approach offers several advantages:

- Efficiency: By summarizing the conversation, it reduces the amount of information the LLM needs to process, improving performance, especially for long conversations.
- Focus on Key Information: The summary highlights the most important aspects of the conversation, allowing the LLM to focus on the key points.[2]
- Reduced Token Consumption: Summaries typically use fewer tokens than the full conversation history, which can be important when working with LLMs that have token limits or cost associated with token usage.[3]

Code Example (Python with LangChain)

```python
from langchain.chains import ConversationChain
from langchain.llms import OpenAI
from langchain.memory import ConversationSummaryMemory
```
[4]

```python
# Initialize the LLM and memory
llm = OpenAI(temperature=0)
memory = ConversationSummaryMemory(llm=llm)  # Use an LLM for summarization

# Create the conversation chain with memory
conversation = ConversationChain(llm=llm, memory=memory, verbose=True)

# Start the conversation
conversation.predict(input="Hi, my name is Bob.")
```

```
conversation.predict(input="I'm interested in
learning about space exploration.")

conversation.predict(input="Can you tell me more
about the Mars rover missions?")
```

In this example, ConversationSummaryMemory uses the LLM to create a summary of the conversation after each turn. This summary is then included in the context for the next interaction, allowing the LLM to remember that Bob is interested in space exploration even though the initial message is not included in the full context.

Customization Options

ConversationSummaryMemory offers some customization options:

- llm: You can specify the LLM to use for summarization.[5]
- prompt: You can provide a custom prompt to guide the summarization process.

Real-World Examples

- Customer Support: For chatbots that handle complex customer issues, ConversationSummaryMemory can help maintain context and avoid repetition, leading to more efficient and satisfactory resolutions.
- Meeting Summarization: An LLM agent with ConversationSummaryMemory can summarize meeting transcripts, highlighting key decisions, action items, and discussion points.
- Personalized Recommendations: An e-commerce platform can use ConversationSummaryMemory to remember a user's preferences and provide more relevant product recommendations.

Benefits of ConversationSummaryMemory

- Efficiency: Handles long conversations effectively by summarizing the history.[6]
- Focus: Highlights key information for the LLM.[7]
- Reduced Token Usage: Minimizes token consumption, which can be important for cost and performance.[8]

Entity Memory

EntityMemory focuses on storing and retrieving information about specific entities. An entity could be anything that has distinct characteristics or attributes, such as:

- People: Names, ages, professions, addresses, etc.
- Objects: Products, items, locations, with their properties and descriptions.
- Concepts: Ideas, topics, or categories with their associated details.

When you use EntityMemory, you essentially create a knowledge base where you can store and retrieve information about these entities. This allows the LLM to access and use this information in its interactions, providing more personalized and contextually relevant responses.

Key Features

- Specificity: Focuses on storing information about specific entities, making it efficient for retrieving targeted details.
- Structured Information: Stores information in a structured format, typically as key-value pairs or attributes associated with an entity.
- Personalization: Enables highly personalized interactions by remembering details about specific users or objects.

Code Example (Python with LangChain)

```python
from langchain.chains import ConversationChain
from langchain.llms import OpenAI
from langchain.memory import ConversationEntityMemory[1]

# Initialize the LLM and memory
llm = OpenAI(temperature=0)
memory = ConversationEntityMemory()

# Create the conversation chain with memory
conversation = ConversationChain(llm=llm, memory=memory, verbose=True)

# Start the conversation
conversation.predict(input="My favorite color is blue.")
conversation.predict(input="What's my favorite color?")
```

In this example, ConversationEntityMemory stores the user's favorite color as an attribute associated with the user entity. When asked about their favorite color, the LLM can access the memory and retrieve the correct answer.

Real-World Examples

- Customer Support: A chatbot can use EntityMemory to remember customer details, such as their order history, preferences, and past issues, providing more personalized and efficient support.

- Personalized Recommendations: An e-commerce platform can use EntityMemory to remember user preferences, purchase history, and product ratings to provide tailored recommendations.
- Game AI: A game AI can use EntityMemory to remember the player's actions, inventory, and progress, creating a more immersive and personalized gaming experience.

Benefits of Entity Memory

- Personalization: Provides highly personalized interactions by remembering details about specific entities.
- Efficiency: Efficiently retrieves specific information about entities, avoiding the need to process the entire conversation history.
- Contextual Awareness: Allows the LLM to understand the context of the conversation by accessing relevant information about the entities involved.

Advanced Usage

You can further enhance EntityMemory by:

- Custom Entity Extraction: Use custom functions or LLMs to extract entities and their attributes from the conversation.
- External Knowledge Bases: Connect EntityMemory to external knowledge bases or databases to access a wider range of information about entities.

5.3 Integrating Memory into LLM Applications

Integrating memory is like giving your LLMs a superpower, enabling them to have more meaningful and engaging conversations. Let's explore how to seamlessly add this capability to your projects.

Why Integrate Memory?

As we discussed earlier, memory is essential for creating LLM applications that can:

- Maintain context in conversations
- Personalize interactions
- Exhibit consistent behavior
- Learn and adapt over time

By integrating memory, you can transform your LLMs from simple input-output machines into more intelligent and interactive conversational partners.

Steps to Integrate Memory with LangChain

LangChain makes it remarkably easy to add memory to your LLM applications. Here's a step-by-step guide:

1. **Choose the Right Memory Type:**

LangChain offers various memory types, each with its own strengths and weaknesses:

- ConversationBufferMemory: Stores the entire conversation history.
- ConversationSummaryMemory: Keeps a summarized version of the conversation.
- ConversationEntityMemory: Remembers specific entities and their attributes.

Select the memory type that best suits your application's needs. Consider factors like the length of the conversations, the type of information you need to store, and the performance requirements.

2. **Initialize the Memory:**

Once you've chosen a memory type, create an instance of the corresponding class. For example:

Python

```
from langchain.memory import ConversationBufferMemory
memory = ConversationBufferMemory()
```

3. **Attach the Memory to Your LLM Chain or Agent:**

LangChain provides a straightforward way to attach memory to your LLM chains or agents. Simply pass the memory object as an argument when creating the chain or agent. For example:

Python

```
from langchain.chains import ConversationChain
from langchain.llms import OpenAI
llm = OpenAI(temperature=0)
conversation = ConversationChain(llm=llm, memory=memory)
```

4. **(Optional) Customize the Memory:**

Some memory types offer customisations options. For example, with ConversationSummaryMemory, you can specify the LLM to use for summarization or provide a custom prompt. Explore the documentation for the specific memory type you're using to see what customization options are available.

Code Example: Building a Chatbot with Memory

Let's put these steps into action by building a simple chatbot that remembers the user's name and favorite color:

Python

```
from langchain.chains import ConversationChain
from langchain.llms import OpenAI
from langchain.memory import ConversationEntityMemory[1]

# Initialize the LLM and memory
llm = OpenAI(temperature=0)
memory = ConversationEntityMemory()

# Create the conversation chain with memory
conversation = ConversationChain(llm=llm, memory=memory, verbose=True)

# Start the conversation
conversation.predict(input="My name is Sarah and my favorite color is green.")
conversation.predict(input="What's my favorite color?")
conversation.predict(input="What's my name?")
```

In this example, ConversationEntityMemory stores the user's name and favorite color. The LLM can then access this information to answer the user's questions.

Real-World Examples

- Personalized News Feeds: A news aggregator can use memory to remember a user's preferred topics and sources, providing a personalized news feed.

- Interactive Games: A game can use memory to remember the player's progress, choices, and inventory, creating a more immersive and personalized gaming experience.
- Virtual Assistants: A virtual assistant can use memory to remember user preferences, appointments, and tasks, providing proactive and helpful assistance.

Benefits of Integrating Memory

- Enhanced User Experience: Memory leads to more engaging, personalized, and human-like interactions.
- Improved Accuracy and Consistency: Memory helps LLMs maintain context and avoid contradictions, leading to more accurate and consistent responses.
- Increased Efficiency: Memory allows LLMs to learn from past interactions and improve their performance over time.

5.4 Example: Building a Chatbot with Memory

Building a chatbot is a classic example of how memory can enhance LLM applications, making interactions more engaging and personalized. Imagine interacting with a chatbot that forgets your name or repeats the same questions over and over. It would be a frustrating and impersonal experience. Memory allows chatbots to remember past interactions, user preferences, and important details, creating a more human-like and satisfying conversation.

Building a Chatbot with LangChain

LangChain provides the tools and framework to easily build chatbots with memory. Here's a step-by-step guide:

1. **Choose a Memory Type:**

Select the memory type that best suits your chatbot's needs. For this example, let's use ConversationBufferMemory to store the entire conversation history.

2. **Initialize the LLM and Memory:**

Python

```
from langchain.llms import OpenAI

from langchain.memory import ConversationBufferMemory

llm = OpenAI(temperature=0)

memory = ConversationBufferMemory()[1]
```

3. **Create a Conversation Chain:**

LangChain's ConversationChain provides a convenient way to build chatbots.

```
from langchain.chains import ConversationChain

conversation = ConversationChain(llm=llm, memory=memory, verbose=True)[2]
```

4. **Start the Conversation:**

You can now interact with the chatbot by providing input text.

```python
conversation.predict(input="Hi, my name is Alex.")
```

```python
conversation.predict(input="How are you doing today?")

conversation.predict(input="What was my name again?")
```

Code Example: A Chatbot with Memory

```python
Python

from langchain.chains import ConversationChain

from langchain.llms import OpenAI

from langchain.memory import ConversationBufferMemory
```
[3]

```python
# Initialize the LLM and memory

llm = OpenAI(temperature=0)

memory = ConversationBufferMemory()

# Create the conversation chain with memory

conversation = ConversationChain(llm=llm, memory=memory, verbose=True)

# Start the conversation

conversation.predict(input="Hi, my name is Alex.")

conversation.predict(input="How are you doing today?")

conversation.predict(input="What was my name again?")
```

In this example, the chatbot will remember that the user's name is Alex and use that information in subsequent interactions.

Enhancing the Chatbot

You can further enhance this chatbot by:

- Using Different Memory Types: Experiment with ConversationSummaryMemory or ConversationEntityMemory to see how they affect the chatbot's behavior.
- Adding Personality: Guide the LLM to adopt a specific personality or tone of voice through prompt engineering.
- Incorporating Tools: Add tools to enable the chatbot to perform tasks, such as web search, calendar access, or information retrieval.
- Improving the User Interface: Integrate the chatbot with a messaging platform or create a graphical user interface for a more interactive experience.

Real-World Examples

- Customer Support: Companies use chatbots with memory to provide personalized customer support, remembering past issues and preferences.
- Virtual Assistants: Virtual assistants like Siri or Alexa use memory to remember user preferences, schedules, and contacts.
- Educational Chatbots: Educational chatbots can use memory to track student progress, provide personalized feedback, and adapt the learning experience.

Benefits of Chatbots with Memory

- Personalized Experience: Memory allows chatbots to provide a more personalized and engaging experience for users.

- Improved Efficiency: Chatbots with memory can handle more complex conversations and provide more relevant information.
- Increased User Satisfaction: Users are more likely to be satisfied with chatbots that remember their preferences and past interactions.

By building chatbots with memory using LangChain, you can create more intelligent and interactive conversational agents that can provide valuable services and enhance user experiences.

Chapter 6: Case Studies and Practical Examples

We've covered the core concepts of LangChain—now let's discuss how they can be applied to build real-world applications. These case studies will give you a taste of what's possible and inspire you to create your own LLM-powered solutions.

6.1 Building a Chatbot with LangChain

Chatbots are everywhere these days, and LangChain provides the perfect toolkit to build ones that are more engaging, helpful, and personalized than ever before.

Traditional chatbots often rely on pre-defined rules and scripts, limiting their ability to handle diverse conversations and provide truly helpful responses. With LangChain, you can create chatbots that go beyond these limitations.

Key Features of Advanced Chatbots

- Natural Language Understanding: They can understand the nuances of human language, including slang, idioms, and complex sentence structures.
- Contextual Awareness: They can remember past interactions and user preferences, providing more relevant and personalized responses.
- Task Completion: They can perform actions, such as answering questions, providing information, or even completing tasks like booking appointments or ordering products.
- Adaptability: They can learn and adapt to new information and user preferences over time.

Building Blocks of a LangChain Chatbot

Here are the essential components for building a sophisticated chatbot with LangChain:

1. **Large Language Model (LLM):** This is the brain of your chatbot, responsible for understanding and generating human language. Choose an LLM that suits your needs, such as OpenAI's GPT models, a model from Hugging Face, or any other LLM supported by LangChain.
2. **Memory:** Memory is crucial for giving your chatbot a sense of context and allowing it to remember past interactions. LangChain offers various memory types, such as:
    - ConversationBufferMemory: Stores the entire conversation history.
    - ConversationSummaryMemory: Keeps a summarized version of the conversation.
    - ConversationEntityMemory: Remembers specific entities and their attributes.
3. **Chains:** Chains allow you to create more complex conversational flows. You can use chains to:
    - Handle multi-turn dialogues.
    - Incorporate external actions, such as searching the web or accessing a database.
    - Combine multiple LLMs or tools to perform different tasks.
4. **Tools:** Tools give your chatbot the ability to interact with the world beyond language. Examples of tools include:
    - google_search: For searching the web.
    - python_repl: For executing Python code.
    - requests: For interacting with APIs.

Code Example (Python with LangChain)

```Python
from langchain.agents import load_tools

from langchain.agents import initialize_agent
```

```python
from langchain.agents import AgentType

from langchain.llms import OpenAI[1]

from langchain.memory import ConversationSummaryMemory[2]

# Load the Google Search tool

tools = load_tools(["google_search"], llm=OpenAI(temperature=0))

# Initialize the LLM and memory

llm = OpenAI(temperature=0)

memory = ConversationSummaryMemory(llm=llm)

# Initialize the agent

agent = initialize_agent(
    tools,
    llm,
    agent=AgentType.ZERO_SHOT_REACT_DESCRIPTION,
    verbose=True,
    memory=memory,
)

# Start the conversation

agent.run("Hi, my name is Emily. Can you tell me about the history of the internet?")
```

```
agent.run("That's fascinating! Can you find some
articles about the early pioneers of the
internet?")
```

In this example, the chatbot uses the Google Search tool to find information about the history of the internet and remembers the user's name and previous request.

Real-World Applications

Chatbots built with LangChain can be used in various domains:

- Customer Support: Provide 24/7 support, answer questions, resolve issues, and collect customer feedback.
- E-commerce: Guide customers through product selection, provide personalized recommendations, and process orders.
- Education: Tutor students, answer questions, provide personalized learning experiences, and assess their understanding.
- Healthcare: Provide medical information, schedule appointments, answer patient questions, and assist with administrative tasks.
- Human Resources: Answer employee questions, assist with onboarding processes, and provide information about company policies.

Benefits of Building Chatbots with LangChain

- Enhanced User Experience: Create more engaging and personalized conversations.
- Increased Efficiency: Automate customer support and other tasks.
- Improved Accuracy: Provide more accurate and comprehensive information by accessing external knowledge sources.
- Scalability: Handle a large volume of conversations simultaneously.

6.2 Creating a Question-Answering System

Question-answering systems are becoming increasingly important in various domains, from customer service to education and research. Let's explore how to build a robust and effective question-answering system using LangChain.

Traditional question-answering systems often rely on keyword matching or rule-based approaches, which can be limited in their ability to handle complex questions or provide nuanced answers. With LLMs and LangChain, you can create more sophisticated systems that can:

- Understand Complex Questions: Interpret questions that involve multiple concepts, relationships, or constraints.
- Provide Context-Aware Answers: Consider the context of the question, the user's previous interactions, and the specific domain of knowledge.
- Explain Their Reasoning: Provide explanations or justifications for their answers, increasing transparency and trust.
- Access and Synthesize Information: Retrieve information from various sources, such as documents, databases, or the web, and synthesize it to provide comprehensive answers.

Key Components of a Question-Answering System

1. Large Language Model (LLM): The LLM is the core of your system, responsible for understanding questions and generating answers. Choose an LLM with strong language understanding and reasoning capabilities, such as OpenAI's GPT models or other LLMs specialized in question answering.
2. Retrieval System: A retrieval system is crucial for finding relevant information from a knowledge base. This could be

a collection of documents, a database, or even the web. Some common retrieval systems include:
- FAISS: A library for efficient similarity search and clustering of vectors.
- Elasticsearch: A powerful search engine that can handle various data types and search queries.
- LangChain's built-in document loaders: For loading and processing documents from different sources.

3. Chains: Chains allow you to orchestrate the question-answering process. You can use chains to:
   - Retrieve relevant documents or information from the knowledge base.
   - Extract key information from the retrieved documents.
   - Generate an answer based on the extracted information and the original question.

4. Memory (Optional): Memory can enhance the question-answering system by allowing it to:
   - Remember previous questions and answers.
   - Track the user's interests and preferences.
   - Maintain context across multiple interactions.

Code Example (Python with LangChain)

```python
from langchain.chains.question_answering import load_qa_chain

from langchain.llms import OpenAI

from langchain.docstore.simple_docstore[1] import SimpleDocstore

# Create a simple document store
docs = [
    {
```

```
        "source": "document 1",
        "page_content": "The capital of France is Paris.",
    },
    {
        "source": "document 2",
        "page_content": "The Eiffel Tower is located in Paris.",
    },
]
docstore = SimpleDocstore(docs)
# Initialize the LLM and QA chain
llm = OpenAI(temperature=0)
chain = load_qa_chain(llm, chain_type="stuff")
# Ask a question
query = "Where is the Eiffel Tower located?"
answer = chain.run(input_documents=docstore.search(query), question=query)
print(answer)
```

In this example, we create a simple document store and use a pre-built question-answering chain from LangChain to answer the question. The chain retrieves relevant documents from the store and generates an answer based on the information found.

Real-World Examples

- Customer Support: Companies use question-answering systems to provide instant answers to customer questions about products, services, or policies.

- Research: Researchers use question-answering systems to quickly find relevant information from scientific papers, legal documents, or historical archives.
- Education: Educational platforms use question-answering systems to provide students with answers to their questions, explanations of concepts, and personalized feedback.
- Knowledge Management: Organizations use question-answering systems to make internal knowledge more accessible to employees, improving productivity and decision-making.

Benefits of Using LangChain for Question Answering

- Flexibility: LangChain allows you to easily customize and adapt your question-answering system to different domains and use cases.
- Efficiency: LangChain provides pre-built chains and tools that simplify the development process.
- Scalability: LangChain can handle large knowledge bases and high volumes of queries.
- Integration: LangChain can be easily integrated with other systems and applications.

6.3 Developing a Code Assistant

Code assistants are transforming the way developers write code, boosting productivity and making coding more accessible to everyone. Let's see how you can use LangChain to build your own powerful code assistant.

Traditional code editors often provide basic code completion features, suggesting possible completions based on the current context. But with LLMs and LangChain, you can create code assistants that go far beyond that.

Key Features of Advanced Code Assistants

- Code Generation from Natural Language: Allow developers to describe what they want the code to do in plain English, and the assistant generates the corresponding code.
- Code Explanation: Provide clear explanations and documentation for existing code, making it easier to understand and maintain.
- Code Refactoring: Suggest improvements to code structure, readability, and efficiency.
- Code Debugging: Help identify and fix errors in code, saving developers time and frustration.
- Code Translation: Translate code from one programming language to another.
- Code Completion: Provide more intelligent and context-aware code completions.

Building Blocks of a Code Assistant with LangChain

1. Large Language Model (LLM): Choose an LLM with strong code generation capabilities. Some popular options include:
   - Codex: OpenAI's LLM specifically trained on code.
   - Codegen: Salesforce's code generation model.
   - Other LLMs fine-tuned on code: Many LLMs can be fine-tuned on code datasets to improve their code generation abilities.
2. Code Interpreter (Optional): A code interpreter allows the LLM to execute code and see the results. This can be useful for tasks like debugging or generating code that interacts with external systems.
3. Tools: Integrate tools to give your code assistant access to relevant resources. Examples of tools include:
   - Code repositories: Access to GitHub, GitLab, or other code repositories.
   - Documentation: Access to programming language documentation, API references, and tutorials.
   - Code analysis tools: Integration with linters, formatters, and other code analysis tools.

4. Chains: Use chains to orchestrate the code assistance process. You can use chains to:
    - Generate code from natural language descriptions.
    - Analyze code and provide explanations or suggestions.
    - Combine multiple LLMs or tools to perform different code-related tasks.

Code Example (Python with LangChain)

```python
from langchain.llms import OpenAI
from langchain.prompts import PromptTemplate
# Initialize the LLM
llm = OpenAI(temperature=0)
# Define the prompt template
template = """
You are a helpful assistant that writes Python code.
### Instructions:
{instructions}
### Code:
"""
prompt_template = PromptTemplate(input_variables=["instructions"], template=template)
# Generate code from natural language instructions
```

```
instructions = "Write a function that takes a
list of numbers and returns the sum of all the
even numbers in the list."
prompt =
prompt_template.format(instructions=instructions)
code = llm(prompt)
print(code)
```

In this example, we use a prompt template to guide the LLM to generate Python code based on natural language instructions.

Real-World Examples

- GitHub Copilot: A code assistant developed by GitHub and OpenAI that provides code suggestions and completions in real-time.
- Tebnine: A code completion tool that uses LLMs to provide intelligent suggestions.
- Replit Ghostwriter: A code generation and debugging tool integrated into the Replit online IDE.

Benefits of Code Assistants

- Increased Productivity: Automate repetitive coding tasks and generate code faster.
- Improved Code Quality: Generate code that adheres to best practices and coding standards.
- Reduced Errors: Help identify and fix errors in code.
- Enhanced Learning: Provide explanations and examples to help developers learn new concepts and techniques.
- Accessibility: Make coding more accessible to people with less experience.

6.4 Generating Personalized Content

Personalized content is a powerful way to engage users, whether it's through customized marketing messages, individualized learning materials, or unique creative pieces. LLMs, combined with LangChain, are revolutionizing how we generate this content.

Why Personalization Matters

In today's world, people expect experiences that are relevant to their individual needs and preferences. Generic, one-size-fits-all content often falls flat. Personalized content, on the other hand, can:

- Increase Engagement: People are more likely to pay attention to content that is relevant to their interests and needs.
- Improve User Experience: Tailored content creates a more satisfying and enjoyable experience for users.
- Drive Conversions: Personalized marketing messages are more likely to lead to conversions, whether it's a purchase, a sign-up, or another desired action.
- Foster Loyalty: People are more likely to remain loyal to brands and platforms that provide personalized experiences.

Types of Personalized Content

LLMs can generate a wide range of personalized content, including:

Marketing Materials:

- Emails: Tailored subject lines, product recommendations, and promotional offers.
- Social Media Posts: Engaging content that resonates with individual users' interests.

- Advertisements: Targeted ads that match user demographics and preferences.

Educational Content:

- Learning Plans: Customized learning paths based on a student's strengths and weaknesses.
- Study Materials: Adaptive exercises and explanations that adjust to the student's level of understanding.
- Feedback: Personalized feedback on assignments and assessments.

Creative Content:

- Stories: Stories with characters, settings, and plots tailored to the reader's preferences.
- Poems: Poems that reflect the reader's emotions, experiences, or interests.
- Music: Generated music that matches the listener's preferred style and mood.

Building Blocks for Personalized Content Generation

1. Large Language Model (LLM): Choose an LLM with strong text generation capabilities and the ability to adapt to different styles and tones.
2. User Profiles: Gather information about user preferences, interests, and history. This data can be collected through:
    - Explicit Feedback: Surveys, questionnaires, and preference settings.
    - Implicit Feedback: Website interactions, purchase history, and content consumption patterns.
    - External Data: Demographic data, social media profiles, and other publicly available information.
3. Dynamic Prompts: Use dynamic prompts to incorporate user information into the LLM's input. This allows you to tailor the generated content to each individual user.

4. **Content Library (Optional):** If you're generating content based on a pre-existing collection of materials, such as articles, product descriptions, or learning resources, you'll need a content library that can be easily accessed and filtered.

Code Example (Python with LangChain)

```python
from langchain.llms import OpenAI
from langchain.prompts import PromptTemplate

# Initialize the LLM
llm = OpenAI(temperature=0.7)

# Define the prompt template with user-specific variables
template = """
Write a short story for {user_name} about a {user_interest}.
"""

prompt_template = PromptTemplate(
    input_variables=["user_name", "user_interest"], template=template
)

# Generate personalized content
user_name = "Alice"
```

```
user_interest = "talking cat"

prompt = prompt_template.format(user_name=user_name,
user_interest=user_interest)

story = llm(prompt)

print(story)
```

In this example, we use a dynamic prompt to generate a personalized story for a user named Alice who is interested in talking cats.

Real-World Examples

- Netflix: Uses personalized recommendations to suggest movies and shows based on user viewing history and preferences.
- Spotify: Creates personalized playlists and music recommendations based on user listening habits.
- Amazon: Provides personalized product recommendations and targeted advertisements based on user browsing and purchase history.
- Duolingo: Adapts language learning exercises and feedback to individual student needs and progress.

Benefits of Generating Personalized Content with LLMs

- Increased Engagement: Capture user attention with relevant and interesting content.
- Improved User Experience: Create a more satisfying and enjoyable experience.
- Better Conversions: Drive desired actions with targeted messaging.
- Enhanced Loyalty: Foster stronger relationships with users by providing personalized experiences.

6.5 Automating Customer Support

Customer support is a critical function for any business, and automating it with LLMs can lead to significant improvements in efficiency, cost-effectiveness, and customer satisfaction.[1]

Traditional customer support often involves human agents handling a high volume of inquiries through various channels like phone, email, and chat. This can be:

- Costly: Hiring and training human agents can be expensive.
- Time-consuming: Resolving complex issues can take a significant amount of time.[2]
- Inconsistent: Different agents may provide different answers or levels of service.
- Limited Availability: Human agents are not available 24/7.

How LLMs Can Transform Customer Support

LLMs, combined with LangChain, can automate many aspects of customer support, leading to:[3]

- 24/7 Availability: LLM-powered systems can provide support around the clock, regardless of time zones or holidays.[4]
- Faster Response Times: LLMs can instantly analyze customer queries and provide quick responses.[5]
- Consistent Service: LLMs provide consistent answers and follow established procedures.[6]
- Reduced Costs: Automating tasks with LLMs can reduce the need for human agents, leading to cost savings.[7]
- Personalized Support: LLMs can analyze customer data and provide personalized solutions.[8]

Building Blocks of an Automated Customer Support System

1. Large Language Model (LLM): Choose an LLM with strong language understanding, question-answering, and problem-solving capabilities.
2. Knowledge Base: Create a comprehensive knowledge base of FAQs, product information, troubleshooting guides, and other relevant information.[9] This could be in the form of:
    - Documents: Articles, manuals, and tutorials.
    - Databases: Structured data containing product specifications, customer information, and order history.
    - APIs: Access to external systems that provide relevant information, such as shipping status or inventory levels.[10]
3. Tools: Integrate tools to give your customer support system access to relevant information and functionalities. Examples of tools include:
    - Customer Relationship Management (CRM) systems: Access customer data, purchase history, and support interactions.[11]
    - Order management systems: Track order status, process refunds, and handle shipping inquiries.[12]
    - Payment gateways: Process payments and handle billing inquiries.[13]
4. Chains: Use chains to orchestrate the customer support workflow. You can use chains to:
    - Analyze customer queries and identify the intent.[14]
    - Retrieve relevant information from the knowledge base or external systems.
    - Generate helpful responses or solutions.
    - Escalate complex issues to human agents when necessary.[15]

Code Example (Python with LangChain)

Python

```python
from langchain.chains import ConversationChain

from langchain.llms import OpenAI

from langchain.memory import ConversationBufferMemory[16]

# Initialize the LLM and memory

llm = OpenAI(temperature=0)

memory = ConversationBufferMemory()

# Create a conversation chain with a prompt that encourages helpfulness

conversation = ConversationChain(
    llm=llm,
    memory=memory,
    prompt="You are a helpful customer support agent."
)

# Start the conversation

conversation.predict(input="I'm having trouble logging into my account.")

conversation.predict(input="I've tried resetting my password, but it's not working.")
```

In this example, the chatbot uses the provided prompt and its memory of the conversation to assist the user with their login issue.

Real-World Examples

- Chatbots on Websites: Many websites use LLM-powered chatbots to provide instant support, answer questions, and guide users through common tasks.[17]
- Email Support Automation: LLMs can analyze incoming support emails, categorize them, and generate automated responses or route them to the appropriate human agent.[18]
- Social Media Support: LLMs can monitor social media channels for customer inquiries and provide timely responses.[19]
- Voice Assistants: Voice assistants like Siri and Alexa can handle basic customer support inquiries, such as providing information about products or services.[20]

Benefits of Automating Customer Support with LLMs

- Improved Customer Satisfaction: Provide faster and more personalized support.[21]
- Increased Efficiency: Reduce the workload on human agents and allow them to focus on more complex issues.[22]
- Cost Savings: Reduce the cost of customer support by automating tasks.[23]
- Scalability: Handle a large volume of inquiries without compromising service quality.[24]
- Data-Driven Insights: Gather data on customer interactions to identify common issues and improve products or services.[25]

By automating customer support with LLMs and LangChain, businesses can provide a better customer experience, improve efficiency, and gain a competitive advantage.[26]

Chapter 7: Advanced Topics

This chapter explores some of the more advanced aspects of working with LLMs and LangChain, taking your skills to the next level and preparing you for real-world deployment and challenges.

7.1 Evaluation and Fine-tuning of LLM Applications

Building an LLM application is just the beginning. To ensure it truly shines and meets your specific needs, you need to evaluate its performance and fine-tune it for optimal results.

Evaluation

Think of evaluation as a quality control check for your LLM application. It's like giving it a series of exams to assess its capabilities and identify areas for improvement.

Steps in Evaluation

1. Define Metrics: First, you need to determine what constitutes "good" performance for your application. This means identifying the key metrics that are important to you. These might include:
    - Accuracy: How often does the LLM produce correct and factual outputs?
    - Relevance: How well do the LLM's responses address the user's queries or prompts?
    - Fluency: How natural and grammatically correct is the LLM's generated text?
    - Conciseness: How concise and to-the-point are the LLM's responses?
    - Bias: Does the LLM exhibit any biases in its outputs?

- Toxicity: Does the LLM generate any harmful or offensive content?
2. Create Test Datasets: Next, you need to create a set of test data that your LLM application can be evaluated on. This test data should be representative of the real-world scenarios your application will encounter. For example, if you're building a customer service chatbot, your test data might include a variety of customer questions and complaints.
3. Measure Performance: Run your LLM application on the test data and measure its performance against the defined metrics. This might involve calculating accuracy scores, measuring response times, or using human evaluators to assess the quality of the outputs.
4. Analyze Results: Carefully analyze the evaluation results to identify areas where the application is performing well and areas where it needs improvement. This analysis will guide your fine-tuning efforts.

Fine-tuning

Fine-tuning is like taking a general-purpose LLM and giving it specialized training to excel in a particular area. It's a powerful technique for improving the performance and effectiveness of your LLM applications.

Steps in Fine-tuning

1. Choose a Pre-trained LLM: Start with a pre-trained LLM that has a strong foundation in general language understanding. This provides a good starting point for fine-tuning.
2. Create a Fine-tuning Dataset: Prepare a dataset of examples that are specific to the task or domain you want to fine-tune the LLM for. This dataset should be carefully curated to ensure it's representative and of high quality.

3. Train the LLM: Use the fine-tuning dataset to train the LLM, adjusting its parameters to optimize its performance on the specific task. This typically involves using specialized hardware and software for training large language models.
4. Evaluate the Fine-tuned LLM: Once the fine-tuning process is complete, evaluate the performance of the fine-tuned LLM to ensure it has improved. You can use the same evaluation metrics and test datasets that you used for the initial evaluation.

Why Evaluation and Fine-tuning are Crucial

- Improved Performance: Fine-tuning can significantly improve the accuracy, relevance, and overall quality of your LLM application.
- Reduced Bias: Fine-tuning can help mitigate bias in the LLM's output by training it on a more diverse and representative dataset.
- Customization: Fine-tuning allows you to customize the LLM to your specific needs and preferences, such as a particular writing style or tone of voice.
- Efficiency: Fine-tuning can make your LLM application more efficient by reducing the need for complex prompts or chains.

Real-World Examples

- Customer Service: A company fine-tunes an LLM on its customer support conversations to improve the chatbot's ability to understand customer inquiries and provide helpful responses.
- Content Creation: A marketing team fine-tunes an LLM on its product descriptions and marketing materials to generate more engaging and persuasive content that aligns with the company's brand voice.

- Code Generation: A software development team fine-tunes an LLM on its codebase to improve the accuracy and efficiency of its code assistant, allowing it to generate more relevant code suggestions and identify potential errors.

7.2 Integrating LLMs with External Data Sources and APIs

You're looking at a key technique for supercharging your LLM applications! By connecting LLMs to external data sources and APIs, you can give them access to a vast amount of real-world knowledge and functionality, making them far more powerful and versatile.

LLMs, while impressive, are limited by the data they were trained on. This training data might be outdated or lack specific information relevant to your application. Integrating with external data sources allows your LLM to:

- Access Up-to-Date Information: Retrieve current information from the web, databases, or APIs, ensuring your LLM's responses are timely and relevant.
- Expand Knowledge: Access specialized knowledge or data that wasn't included in the LLM's original training data.
- Perform Actions: Interact with external systems to perform actions, such as sending emails, processing payments, or controlling devices.
- Personalize Experiences: Access user-specific data to provide personalized responses and recommendations.

Types of External Data Sources

LLMs can be integrated with a wide variety of external data sources, including:

- Databases: Connect to SQL databases, NoSQL databases, or cloud-based data stores to retrieve structured information.
- APIs: Interact with web APIs to access data and services from various providers, such as social media platforms, weather services, or financial institutions.
- Files: Read and process data from files, such as text files, CSV files, JSON files, or even PDFs.
- Knowledge Graphs: Utilize knowledge graphs, which are structured representations of knowledge, to enable reasoning and inference.

Methods for Integration

LangChain offers several ways to integrate LLMs with external data sources:

- LangChain Tools: LangChain provides a collection of tools designed for accessing specific data sources and APIs. Some examples include:
    - google_search: For searching the web using the Google Search API.
    - python_repl: For executing Python code, which can be used to access databases or interact with APIs.
    - requests: For making HTTP requests to web APIs.
- Custom Tools: You can create your own custom tools to interact with specific data sources or APIs that are not covered by the built-in LangChain tools.
- Agents: LLM agents can be designed to autonomously interact with external systems, retrieve information, and perform actions based on user requests.

Code Example (Python with LangChain)

```python
from langchain.agents import load_tools
from langchain.agents import initialize_agent
```

```python
from langchain.agents import AgentType
from langchain.llms import OpenAI
# Load[1] the Google Search and Python REPL tools
tools = load_tools(["google_search", "python_repl"], llm=OpenAI(temperature=0))
# Initialize the agent
agent = initialize_agent(
    tools,
    OpenAI(temperature=0),
    agent=AgentType.ZERO_SHOT_REACT_DESCRIPTION,
    verbose=True,
)
# Run the agent with a request that requires external data
agent.run("What's the current weather in London, and what is 10 plus 5?")
```

In this example, the agent uses the google_search tool to retrieve the current weather in London and the python_repl tool to perform the calculation.

Real-World Examples

- Financial Analysis: A financial advisor uses an LLM integrated with a stock market API to provide real-time stock quotes, market analysis, and personalized investment recommendations.
- Travel Planning: A travel booking website uses an LLM integrated with flight and hotel APIs to provide users with the best deals and personalized travel itineraries based on their preferences.

- E-commerce: An online store uses an LLM integrated with its product database and a recommendation engine to provide personalized product suggestions, answer customer questions about products, and even generate creative marketing copy.
- Smart Home Automation: A smart home system uses an LLM integrated with various device APIs to control lights, appliances, and thermostats based on natural language commands from the user.

Benefits of Integrating LLMs with External Data

- Real-World Knowledge: LLMs gain access to up-to-date and relevant information from the real world.
- Enhanced Capabilities: LLMs can perform a wider range of tasks and provide more comprehensive responses.
- Personalization: LLMs can access user-specific data to personalize interactions and provide tailored experiences.
- Automation: LLMs can automate tasks and workflows by interacting with external systems.

7.3 Deploying LLM Applications

Deployment is the process of making your LLM application accessible to users.[1] This typically involves setting up the necessary infrastructure, configuring the application, and ensuring it can handle real-world traffic and usage patterns.

Key Considerations for LLM Deployment

1. Scalability: LLM applications, especially those with interactive elements or complex chains, can be resource-intensive.[2] You need to ensure your deployment can handle a large number of users and requests without performance degradation.[3] This might involve using

scalable infrastructure, load balancing, and efficient resource management.
2. Reliability: Your application needs to be reliable and available to users with minimal downtime. This requires careful planning, monitoring, and potentially redundancy measures to ensure continuous operation.[4]
3. Security: Protecting your application and user data is paramount.[5] You need to implement appropriate security measures to prevent unauthorized access, data breaches, and other security threats.[6]
4. Latency: For interactive applications, low latency is crucial for a good user experience.[7] You need to optimize your application and infrastructure to minimize response times and ensure smooth interactions.[8]
5. Cost: Deployment costs can vary depending on the chosen infrastructure, services, and usage patterns.[9] You need to carefully consider cost factors and optimize your deployment to be cost-effective.

Deployment Options

There are several ways to deploy LLM applications:

- Cloud Platforms: Cloud platforms like AWS, Google Cloud, and Azure offer a wide range of services and infrastructure for deploying and scaling applications. They provide flexibility, scalability, and pay-as-you-go pricing models.
- Containerization: Containerization technologies like Docker allow you to package your application and its dependencies into a portable container that can be easily deployed on various platforms.[10]
- Serverless Computing: Serverless platforms like AWS Lambda or Google Cloud Functions allow you to run your application without managing servers.[11] This can be cost-effective and scalable for event-driven applications.

- On-Premise Deployment: For applications with strict security or data privacy requirements, you might choose to deploy on your own servers or infrastructure.

Tools and Frameworks

- LangChain Deployment: LangChain provides tools and integrations for deploying LLM applications on various platforms.
- Cloud Provider SDKs: Cloud providers offer SDKs (Software Development Kits) that make it easier to interact with their services and manage your deployments.
- Monitoring Tools: Tools like Prometheus, Grafana, or cloud provider monitoring services help you track your application's performance, resource usage, and identify potential issues.
- CI/CD Pipelines: Continuous Integration and Continuous Deployment (CI/CD) pipelines automate the deployment process, allowing you to quickly and reliably deploy updates and new features.

Real-World Examples

- Chatbot Deployment: A company deploys its customer support chatbot on a cloud platform, using load balancing to handle a large volume of user interactions.
- API Deployment: A developer deploys an LLM-powered API using serverless computing, allowing other applications to access its functionality on demand.[16]
- Mobile App Deployment: A company deploys an LLM-powered language learning app on the iOS and Android app stores, using cloud storage to store user data and progress.

Best Practices for LLM Deployment

- Start with a Small Scale: Begin with a small-scale deployment to test your application and identify any issues before scaling up.
- Monitor Continuously: Use monitoring tools to track your application's performance and identify any potential problems.[17]
- Automate Deployments: Use CI/CD pipelines to automate the deployment process and ensure consistent and reliable deployments.[18]
- Optimize for Performance: Optimize your code, infrastructure, and resource usage to minimize latency and maximize efficiency.[19]
- Secure Your Application: Implement appropriate security measures to protect your application and user data.[20]

7.4 Scaling LLM Applications

Scaling refers to the ability of your application to handle increasing workloads and user traffic. This might involve handling more requests, processing more data, or supporting more concurrent users.

Challenges of Scaling LLM Applications

LLM applications present unique scaling challenges due to their resource-intensive nature:

- Computational Resources: LLMs, especially large ones, require significant computational power for inference (generating text or performing tasks). As the number of users and requests increases, the computational demands can quickly exceed the capacity of a single machine.
- Data Storage: Many LLM applications involve storing and managing large datasets, such as fine-tuning datasets,

knowledge bases, or user interaction history. Scaling the storage and retrieval of this data can be challenging.
- Latency: Maintaining low latency (response times) is crucial for interactive LLM applications. As the number of users increases, network congestion and server load can increase latency, affecting the user experience.
- Cost: Scaling often involves increased costs for infrastructure, computing resources, and data storage. Optimizing costs while ensuring performance is a key challenge.

Scaling Strategies

There are several strategies you can employ to scale your LLM applications effectively:

1. Optimize Code and Algorithms: Before scaling your infrastructure, ensure your code is optimized for efficiency. This might involve using efficient data structures, minimizing unnecessary computations, and optimizing LLM interactions.
2. Caching: Caching frequently accessed data or LLM responses can significantly reduce latency and computational load. This involves storing the results of expensive operations and retrieving them from the cache when needed, rather than recomputing them.
3. Load Balancing: Distribute incoming traffic across multiple servers or instances to prevent any single server from becoming overloaded. This ensures that no single point of failure exists and that resources are utilized effectively.
4. Horizontal Scaling: Increase the number of servers or instances handling your application to distribute the workload. This is often easier and more cost-effective than vertical scaling (increasing the resources of a single machine).
5. Vertical Scaling: Increase the resources of your existing servers, such as CPU, memory, or storage. This can be

effective for certain types of workloads but can be more expensive and may have limitations.
6. Distributed Computing: For tasks that can be parallelized, use distributed computing frameworks like Apache Spark or Ray to distribute the workload across multiple machines.
7. Cloud-Native Architectures: Leverage cloud-native architectures and services, such as serverless computing, container orchestration, and managed databases, to scale your application dynamically based on demand.

Tools and Technologies

- Cloud Scaling Services: Cloud providers offer services like auto-scaling groups and load balancers that automatically adjust your infrastructure based on traffic patterns.
- Container Orchestration: Tools like Kubernetes help you manage and scale containerized applications, automating deployment, scaling, and networking.
- Caching Systems: Caching systems like Redis or Memcached provide high-performance data storage for caching frequently accessed data.
- Monitoring Tools: Monitoring tools help you track your application's performance, identify bottlenecks, and make informed scaling decisions.

Real-World Examples

- Social Media Platform: A social media platform uses a combination of load balancing, horizontal scaling, and caching to handle millions of user requests and content updates per second.
- E-commerce Website: An e-commerce website uses auto-scaling groups to dynamically adjust the number of servers based on traffic, ensuring optimal performance during peak shopping seasons.

- Research Institution: A research institution uses a distributed computing framework to scale its LLM-powered data analysis platform, allowing it to process massive datasets for scientific research.

Best Practices for Scaling LLM Applications

- Plan for Scalability from the Start: Consider scalability requirements early in the design phase of your application.
- Monitor Performance Regularly: Use monitoring tools to track performance metrics and identify potential scaling bottlenecks.
- Automate Scaling: Use auto-scaling and other automation tools to dynamically adjust your infrastructure based on demand.
- Optimize for Cost: Choose cost-effective scaling strategies and optimize your application to minimize resource usage.
- Test at Scale: Conduct load testing and performance testing to ensure your application can handle the expected traffic.

By understanding the challenges of scaling LLM applications and applying the appropriate strategies and tools, you can ensure your application can handle growth and provide a consistently excellent user experience.

Chapter 8: The Future of LLMs and LangChain

We've covered a lot of ground in this book, from the fundamentals of LLMs to the intricacies of LangChain. The field of LLMs is rapidly evolving, with new advancements and applications emerging all the time. In this final chapter, let's explore what the future holds for LLMs and LangChain, and discuss some important ethical considerations.

8.1 Emerging Trends in the LLM Landscape

The field of Large Language Models (LLMs) is evolving at an incredible pace. It's a fascinating time to be involved in this space, and understanding the emerging trends will help you stay ahead of the curve.

1. The Rise of Multimodal LLMs

While we've mostly focused on text-based LLMs in this book, the future is multimodal. This means that LLMs are becoming increasingly capable of processing and generating information in multiple modalities, such as:

- Text: Understanding and generating written language, as we've already explored.
- Images: Analyzing and generating images, including understanding the content and context of images.
- Audio: Processing and generating speech, music, and other sounds.
- Video: Understanding and generating video content, including analyzing scenes, recognizing objects, and even creating video summaries.

This multimodal capability will unlock a whole new range of applications, such as:

- AI assistants that can understand and respond to visual cues.
- Content creation tools that can generate images, videos, and music from text descriptions.
- Interactive learning environments that combine text, images, and audio for a more engaging experience.
- Accessibility tools that can help people with disabilities interact with technology more easily.

2. Specialization is Key

While general-purpose LLMs like GPT-3 are impressive, there's a growing trend towards specialization. This means fine-tuning LLMs for specific domains or tasks, such as:

- Scientific Research: LLMs that can analyze scientific papers, generate hypotheses, and assist in research discovery.
- Legal Analysis: LLMs that can understand legal documents, extract key information, and provide legal advice.
- Creative Writing: LLMs that excel at generating different forms of creative content, such as stories, poems, and scripts.
- Code Generation: LLMs that can generate code in various programming languages, translate code, and assist in software development.

Specialization allows LLMs to achieve higher accuracy and efficiency in those specific domains, making them more valuable for practical applications.

3. The Quest for Efficiency

As LLMs grow in size and complexity, there's an increasing focus on efficiency. This includes:

- Model Compression: Techniques to reduce the size of LLM models without significantly compromising performance.
- Optimization: Improving the efficiency of LLM algorithms and implementations to reduce computational costs.
- Efficient Training: Developing new training methods that require less data and computational resources.

This focus on efficiency is driven by the need to make LLMs more accessible, affordable, and sustainable.

4. Explainability and Interpretability

One of the challenges with LLMs is their "black box" nature. It can be difficult to understand how they arrive at their outputs or to identify potential biases. There's a growing emphasis on:

- Explainable AI (XAI): Developing techniques to make LLM decision-making more transparent and understandable.
- Interpretability: Researching methods to interpret the internal representations and reasoning processes of LLMs.

This will increase trust in LLMs and make it easier to identify and mitigate potential issues.

5. Increased Accessibility

LLMs are becoming more accessible to a wider audience, thanks to:

- Cloud-Based APIs: Cloud providers offer easy-to-use APIs for accessing powerful LLMs.
- Open-Source Models: Many LLMs are being released as open-source, allowing developers to use and adapt them freely.
- User-Friendly Tools: Tools like LangChain are making it easier for developers to build LLM applications without needing deep expertise in AI.

This increased accessibility will democratize LLMs and empower more people to leverage their capabilities.

Real-World Examples

- Google's LaMDA: A multimodal LLM that can engage in conversations, generate different creative text formats, and even write different kinds of creative content.
- OpenAI's Codex: An LLM specialized in code generation that can translate between programming languages and assist in software development.
- Hugging Face's Transformers library: Provides access to a wide range of open-source LLMs, including specialized models for various tasks.

These emerging trends indicate that the field of LLMs is rapidly advancing, with exciting new possibilities on the horizon. By staying informed about these trends and embracing the principles of responsible AI, you can be a part of this exciting journey and contribute to the development of LLM applications that benefit society.

8.2 Future Directions for LangChain

LangChain has quickly become a popular framework for building LLM applications, but it's not standing still. The developers are actively working to improve and expand its capabilities to keep pace with the rapidly evolving LLM landscape.

One of the key strengths of LangChain is its ability to work with a variety of LLMs. We can expect this support to broaden even further, encompassing:

- More LLMs: LangChain will likely integrate with more LLMs from different providers, including open-source models and those with specialized capabilities. This will give

you greater flexibility and choice in selecting the best LLM for your specific needs.
- Multimodal LLMs: As multimodal LLMs become more prevalent, LangChain will need to adapt to support these models. This might involve new chain types, components, and interfaces that can handle different modalities, such as images, audio, and video.

New Chain Types and Components

LangChain already offers a variety of chain types, but we can anticipate the introduction of new and more sophisticated chains, such as:

- Chains for Multimodal Reasoning: These chains could combine LLMs with other AI models, such as image recognition models or speech-to-text models, to enable reasoning and decision-making across different modalities.
- Planning Chains: These chains could incorporate planning algorithms or LLMs specialized in planning to generate and execute complex plans involving multiple steps and dependencies.
- Interactive Chains: These chains could facilitate more interactive and dynamic conversations with LLMs, allowing for real-time feedback, user input, and adaptation.

Improved Tooling and Integrations

LangChain will likely continue to improve its tooling and integrations to make it even easier to build, deploy, and manage LLM applications. This might include:

- Better Support for Cloud Platforms: Enhanced integrations with cloud providers like AWS, Google Cloud, and Azure, making it easier to deploy and scale LLM applications on these platforms.
- Enhanced Monitoring Tools: Improved tools for monitoring the performance, cost, and usage of LLM applications,

- providing insights to optimize and troubleshoot deployments.
- Streamlined Development Environments: Better integrations with popular code editors and IDEs, making it easier to develop and debug LangChain applications.

Focus on Responsible AI

As LLMs become more powerful, it's crucial to use them responsibly. LangChain can play a role in promoting responsible AI practices by:

- Incorporating Bias Detection and Mitigation Tools: Providing tools that help developers identify and mitigate bias in their LLM applications, ensuring fairness and inclusivity.
- Encouraging Transparency and Explainability: Promoting the use of explainable AI techniques and providing tools for understanding LLM behavior, increasing trust and accountability.
- Facilitating Responsible Fine-tuning: Providing guidance and tools for fine-tuning LLMs in a responsible manner, ensuring that fine-tuned models are aligned with ethical guidelines.

Growing Community and Ecosystem

LangChain has a vibrant and growing community of developers, researchers, and users. This community plays a crucial role in the future of LangChain by:

- Contributing to the Project: Developing new features, fixing bugs, and improving documentation.
- Sharing Knowledge and Best Practices: Creating tutorials, blog posts, and other resources to help others learn and use LangChain effectively.
- Providing Support and Collaboration: Answering questions, offering assistance, and collaborating on projects.

Real-World Examples

While these are future directions, we can already see some of these trends emerging:

- LangChain Hub: A platform for sharing and discovering reusable LangChain components and chains, promoting collaboration and knowledge sharing within the community.
- LangChain Expression Language (LCEL): A new language for defining and executing chains in a more concise and expressive way.
- Integration with Hugging Face Transformers Agents: Allows developers to use Hugging Face Transformers agents within LangChain, expanding the range of available tools and functionalities.

The future of LangChain is bright. By continuing to adapt and evolve with the LLM landscape, LangChain will remain a valuable tool for building innovative and impactful LLM applications. As a user of LangChain, you can contribute to its future by actively participating in the community, sharing your knowledge, and providing feedback to the developers.

8.3 Ethical Considerations and Responsible AI

As we unlock the incredible potential of LLMs and LangChain, it's essential to proceed with caution and awareness. Ethical considerations and responsible AI practices are not just buzzwords; they are fundamental to ensuring that these powerful technologies are used for good and benefit society as a whole.

Why Ethics Matter in AI

LLMs are not simply tools; they are complex systems that can learn, adapt, and make decisions. This gives them the potential to significantly impact individuals and society, both positively and negatively. Ethical considerations help us navigate this complex landscape and ensure that LLMs are developed and used in a way that aligns with our values and promotes human well-being.

Key Ethical Considerations for LLMs

1. **Bias and Fairness:**

LLMs learn from massive datasets, and these datasets can contain biases that reflect societal prejudices or inequalities. If not addressed, these biases can be amplified and perpetuated by LLMs, leading to unfair or discriminatory outcomes.

Mitigation Strategies:

- Careful Data Curation: Use diverse and representative training data that reflects different perspectives and demographics.
- Bias Detection and Mitigation: Develop and employ tools to detect and mitigate bias in training data and LLM outputs.
- Fine-tuning: Fine-tune LLMs on datasets that promote fairness and inclusivity.
- Auditing and Accountability: Regularly audit LLM applications for bias and establish clear accountability mechanisms.

2. **Misinformation and Manipulation:**

LLMs can generate highly convincing and persuasive text, which can be misused to spread misinformation or manipulate people's opinions and behaviors. This raises concerns about the potential for malicious actors to use LLMs for propaganda, fraud, or other harmful purposes.

Mitigation Strategies:

- Content Moderation: Develop and implement robust content moderation policies and tools to identify and flag potentially harmful or misleading content generated by LLMs.
- Source Verification: Encourage LLMs to provide sources and evidence for their claims, and develop methods to verify the authenticity and credibility of information.
- Media Literacy: Promote media literacy and critical thinking skills to help people distinguish between reliable and unreliable information, including content generated by LLMs.

3. **Privacy and Security:**

LLM applications often involve processing sensitive user data, such as personal information, conversations, or preferences. Protecting this data and ensuring user privacy is crucial.

Mitigation Strategies:

- Data Minimization: Collect and store only the necessary user data.
- Data Security: Implement strong security measures to protect user data from unauthorized access and breaches.
- Transparency and Control: Provide users with clear information about how their data is being used and give them control over their data.
- Compliance with Regulations: Adhere to relevant data privacy regulations, such as GDPR or CCPA.

4. Transparency and Explainability:

LLMs can be complex and opaque, making it difficult to understand how they arrive at their outputs. This lack of transparency can lead to mistrust and hinder accountability.

Mitigation Strategies:

- Explainable AI (XAI): Develop and use XAI techniques to make LLM decision-making more transparent and understandable.
- Interpretability Research: Invest in research to better understand the internal workings of LLMs and develop methods to interpret their outputs.
- Clear Communication: Communicate clearly to users how LLMs are being used in the application and provide explanations for their outputs when possible.

5. Job Displacement and Economic Impact:

LLMs have the potential to automate tasks that were previously performed by humans, raising concerns about job displacement and economic inequality.

Mitigation Strategies:

Responsible Automation: Focus on using LLMs to augment human capabilities rather than simply replacing human workers.

Reskilling and Upskilling: Invest in programs to help workers develop new skills and adapt to the changing job market.

Fair Distribution of Benefits: Ensure that the benefits of LLM technology are shared equitably and that the potential negative impacts are mitigated.

The Role of LangChain in Responsible AI

LangChain can be a valuable tool for promoting responsible AI practices by:

- Providing Tools for Bias Detection and Mitigation: LangChain can incorporate tools that help developers identify and mitigate bias in their LLM applications.
- Encouraging Transparency and Explainability: LangChain can promote the use of explainable AI techniques and provide tools for understanding LLM behavior.
- Facilitating Responsible Fine-tuning: LangChain can provide guidance and tools for fine-tuning LLMs in a responsible manner, ensuring that fine-tuned models are fair, unbiased, and aligned with ethical guidelines.
- Fostering a Culture of Responsible AI: The LangChain community can play a role in promoting responsible AI practices and raising awareness of ethical considerations.

Ensuring the ethical and responsible use of LLMs is a shared responsibility among developers, researchers, policymakers, and users. By being mindful of these considerations and actively working to mitigate potential risks, we can harness the power of LLMs for good and create a future where AI benefits everyone.

Conclusion

We've reached the end of our exploration of LangChain and the exciting world of Large Language Models (LLMs). But in many ways, this is just the beginning. The field of LLMs is evolving rapidly, and the possibilities for innovation and impact are truly vast.

Throughout this book, we've journeyed from the fundamentals of LLMs and prompt engineering to the intricacies of chains, agents, and memory. We've explored how to build a variety of applications, from chatbots and question-answering systems to code assistants and personalized content generators. We've also delved into advanced topics like fine-tuning, deployment, and scaling, and addressed the crucial ethical considerations surrounding responsible AI.

Key Takeaways

- LLMs are powerful tools: LLMs have the potential to revolutionize many aspects of our lives, from how we interact with technology to how we solve problems and create new things.
- LangChain simplifies LLM development: LangChain provides a flexible and powerful framework for building LLM applications, making it easier to harness the capabilities of these models.
- Prompt engineering is crucial: The way you communicate with LLMs through prompts significantly impacts the quality and effectiveness of their outputs.
- Chains unlock complex workflows: Chains allow you to combine LLMs and other tools to create sophisticated applications that can perform a wide range of tasks.

- Agents enable autonomous behavior: Agents give LLMs the ability to interact with their environment, make decisions, and achieve goals.
- Memory enhances context and personalization: Memory allows LLMs to remember past interactions and provide more personalized and engaging experiences.
- Responsible AI is essential: As we build and deploy LLM applications, it's crucial to consider the ethical implications and ensure responsible use of these powerful technologies.

The future of LLMs and LangChain is full of promise. We can expect to see even more powerful and versatile LLMs emerge, along with new tools and techniques for building and deploying LLM applications. LangChain will continue to evolve to support these advancements and empower developers to create innovative solutions.

Your Role in the LLM Revolution

As you've learned throughout this book, you have the power to shape the future of LLMs. Whether you're a developer, a researcher, or simply an enthusiast, you can contribute to this exciting field by:

- Building innovative applications: Use your creativity and skills to build LLM applications that solve real-world problems and enhance human experiences.
- Sharing your knowledge: Contribute to the LangChain community, share your experiences, and help others learn and grow.
- Promoting responsible AI: Advocate for the ethical use of LLMs and contribute to the development of responsible AI practices.

The journey with LLMs and LangChain is just beginning. Embrace the opportunities, explore the possibilities, and contribute to the responsible development and use of these transformative technologies. The future is yours to shape.

www.ingramcontent.com/pod-product-compliance
Lightning Source LLC
Chambersburg PA
CBHW082248220526
45469CB00009B/2914